WHAT HAPPENS WHEN I DIE?

To Drew

He is the Lord of Life

WHAT HAPPENS WHEN I DIE ?

DAVID EDWARDS

Building the New Generation of Believers

COOK COMMUNICATIONS MINISTRIES
Colorado Springs, Colorado • Paris, Ontario
KINGSWAY COMMUNICATIONS LTD
Eastbourne, England

NexGen® is an imprint of
Cook Communications Ministries, Colorado Springs, CO 80918
Cook Communications, Paris, Ontario
Kingsway Communications, Eastbourne, England

WHAT HAPPENS WHEN I DIE?
© 2004 by David Edwards

First Printing, 2004
Printed in the United States of America
1 2 3 4 5 6 7 8 9 10 Printing/Year 08 07 06 05 04

Unless otherwise noted Scripture quotations are taken from the NEW
AMERICAN STANDARD BIBLE®, Copyright © 1960, 1962, 1963,
1968, 1971, 1972, 1973, 1975, 1977, 1995 by The Lockman
Foundation. Used by permission.

Cataloging-in-Publication Data on file with the Library of Congress

ISBN 0781441412

To Flipopoly: You've lived life with a godly passion and confidence that has enabled me to see the answers to life that never fail. I'm forever grateful.

To Richard and Marilyn: The heart holds the most important commitments in life. The friendship we share rises to the top of my heart. Thanks for being my committed friends and for helping me know how to answer the questions for life.

CONTENTS

ACKNOWLEDGMENTS

I couldn't have written this book alone. Here are some of the people who helped make it happen.

Trey Bowden: Well, I guess I won't miss a chance to say thank you for your friendship and the great partnership in ministry. Most of all, for watering the rocks in my head.

Janet Lee: You had the vision and insight to set this project in motion. You believed in the value of these books and the impact they will have on thousands of people seeking answers to the questions of life.

Trevor Bron: You took my loaves and fishes and helped multiply them beyond my wildest dreams. A single book becomes a series. Thanks for blessing my life.

Bobby McGraw: I'm still struggling to find your breaking point. Full-time student, pastor—and you still had the time and energy to transcribe this entire project. Wouldn't have happened without you. Your work has been stellar.

Jim Lynch Everybody! You're my friend, my personal doctor who kept me alive—and you drove the comedy engine so well. Better peace through science. Thanks to Eric and Jim Hawkins, for the extra comedy fuel; it helped keep the engine going.

Gary Wilde: Thank you for your surgical editing skills. You preserved the integrity of the manuscripts, communicating the truths that needed to be told, while laughing at my jokes.

Shawn Mathenia: You finally got your very own line in one of my books. *This is it.* Thank you for your friendship and for looking out for me.

Ken Baugh and Frontline: Thank you for your continued passion that shows up in your ongoing work to reach a new generation. You guys are my home away from no home.

The Sound Tracks: Train, Dave Matthews Band, Dave Koz, The Rippingtons, and Journey. Thanks for the inspiration.

The Questions for Life Series

I had just finished speaking at the White House and was eating lunch at Union Station with a young political consultant. We were halfway through our meal when I asked her, "What's life like for a postmodern inside the Beltway? You know, what kinds of questions do they ask?"

"They ask questions about the suffering and wrong in the world," she said, "about the church, and about who Jesus really is. You know, the questions that never fade."

Questions that never fade

Her label for those questions rose up inside of me, and this series of books flowed from that conversation. Postmoderns come wired with the need to answer the questions you'll find in these pages.

Most postmoderns have rejected the pat answers offered by today's spiritual leaders because they have found them to be inadequate for the daily life they face. They have seen others who accepted the ready-made answers but who still struggle making life work. They have no desire to repeat such mistakes. Instead, they challenge the real-life validity of the quick and easy answers.

The questions remain, but some of the questioners let their need for adequate answers diminish into the background. They give way to an apathy that says, "I've got more important things to do in my life than pursuing life's big questions." For others, finding resolution remains a priority. Yet even for them, life can become a never-ending "round-robin" of seeking solutions through new experiences.

Regardless of where you are at the moment, realize that the questions for life never truly fade away. They keep coming back, especially amidst your most trying times. They will keep knocking at your heart's door until you turn and acknowledge their crucial role in finding the life of your dreams. Until you take hold of real explanations, you'll remain constantly searching for the answers that never fail.

Answers that never fail

Spoken or unspoken, identified or unidentified, real answers are priceless. Until we find them, we're haunted by a lack of resolution in life. This unsettled life suffers constant turmoil and never-ending trouble. We look for direction that seems nonexistent, and this makes many of our decisions hard to live with. What price would we pay for a better way?

It's possible to spend a lifetime searching and never finding. Therefore, some would say that the reward comes not in the security of reaching the goal, but in the striving to obtain it. To these people I say: Why waste your life *looking* when you could be *living?*

The Creator of the universe holds the indelible answers we seek. They are not hidden, but they have often been obscured. They are veiled by some who place a higher value on *knowing* the answers than upon allowing the answers to change their lives. We need to push through and ask: What is the actual value of discovering answers that never fail? We'll find the value shining through in *what the answers produce in our lives*. When we discover these answers, our lives change in four supernatural ways. Finding them ...

Builds our outlook It's impossible to live a satisfying life without faith, meaning, and purpose. That's why each of us will place our faith in something or someone that is our primary value. We believe this person or thing will bring meaning and purpose to our life.

Without purpose, we'd have no reason to exist. So even the most cynical and withdrawn person seeks meaning in life. It may reside in something as mundane as keeping a pet iguana fat and happy. Or it could be that he finds meaning in something as twisted as making records and sleeping with young boys.

But life without an ultimate meaning and purpose becomes fragmented and chaotic. We roam from place to place, relationship to relationship, experience to experience, hoping to find something worth living for that endures. The iguana won't live forever. We also quickly discover that people fail us, that work is never-ending, that merely accumulating sensory experiences leads us down a continually darkening pathway.

There is no sense to life without meaning and purpose. There is no meaning and purpose without faith. And there is no faith until we answer the questions that never fade.

Brings ownership Discovering answers to the questions for life transforms us from merely being alive to actually having a life to live. We've all seen people who seem to just take up space in the world. They live for no apparent purpose. The things they do carry no meaning and make no appreciable impact on the people around them. They are alive, but they do not own a life.

> 66 Ownership of life begins when our head and our heart come together at a long-sought crossroads: where the questions that never fade meet the answers that never fail. 99

The questions for life can't be glibly answered, nor should they be made impotent through intellect. They must be answered in our hearts; they must settle down into the very center of our person. Ownership of life begins when our head and our heart come together at a long-sought crossroads: where the questions that never fade meet the answers that never fail.

Breaks us open Every question for life has a spiritual dimension. We may assume that answering the question of world hunger and suffering is only a physical matter, but that would be a wrong assumption. This question first finds its answer in a spiritual dimension, then the physical needs can be addressed in practical action. The same is true for all other questions for life; they each have a spiritual dimension.

The questions for life demand *powerful* answers that remain *present,* regardless of circumstance. The answers that never fade literally open us up to the things of God. That is, they lead us to find and apply his *power* and *presence* to the very heart of our question. These answers don't create despair; they settle disputes. They don't cause confusion; they construct a viable contract between life and us.

Brings an outworking Answering the questions for life develops an internal faith expressed in our observable behaviors. In other words, when we own the answers that never fail, our life takes on a meaning that others see and desire. This outworking of faith is extremely practical. It influences the choices we make, the words we speak, and the attitudes we reflect in daily life.

And this outworking can't help but grow a deep confidence within us. When never-failing solutions calm our internal struggles, we are able to move forward amidst seemingly insurmountable odds. We can work in an environment hostile to the things of Christ—and still live out our faith. We are confident that, although those around us may reject us, we are forever accepted by the One who matters most.

In these books, I have refused to "reheat" the old teachings. Instead of serving leftovers, I've dished up biblical answers that really do apply to the lives we live. These books keep it real, and I've written them with you in mind. I've used generous doses of humor and plenty of anecdotes (most of which actually happened to me).

I've made scant reference to other Christian authors, though, for a reason. In my attempt to make these books fresh, I chose to keep them uncluttered by the thoughts of others. Instead, I try to communicate God's thoughts from the Bible straight to your heart.

You'll notice that the title of each book forms a question. The titles of each chapter also appear as questions. But the content of each chapter *answers* that chapter's question. When read in their entirety, the chapters together answer the big question posed by each book.

You can read these books in any order; they each stand on their own in dealing with a single topic. At the end of each book you'll find questions that I hope will encourage an expanded discussion of the subject matter. Why not bring a group of friends together to talk things through?

Although this book series began over lunch inside the Beltway of Washington, D.C., I am aware that we are all bound together by the questions that never fade. As you read, I hope you will find the answers that never fail.

David Edwards
Summer, 2004

INTRODUCTION TO
WHAT HAPPENS WHEN I DIE?

Halloween used to frighten me as a kid, but it doesn't scare me anymore. To me, it shows just how shallow the Devil really is. But how did the celebration get started? Was there a board meeting in hell? If so, I can just imagine it …

Demons of varying ranks huddle around the long, wrought-iron table, all leaning forward to watch the chair where "he" will soon be seated. These meetings are famous for being unpredictable, so nerves are on edge. "Is it hot in here?" one demon asks, loosening his collar. Before anyone can answer, large metal doors clang open, and in walks the C.E.O.—Chief Evil Operator. He calls the meeting to order and begins.

"I have successfully established my kingdom on earth, and millions are being misled." Gravely voices extend congratulations, everyone preparing for the self-indulgent rant that's sure to follow. "They can now get legal abortions just about everywhere. Sexual abuse has skyrocketed to historic highs. And these pigs are lapping up drugs and alcohol like never before; it makes the Grateful Dead look like the Gaither Homecoming. Ha! They're passing STDs back and forth faster than a Britney Spears marriage. And how about that AIDS!"

Echoes of approval modulate as the boasting continues. "My agenda continues to unfold, and our influence among the human vermin is still strong and viable. I have new plans, too, that will ensure my continued legacy. Of course, I'll give you all the power you need for everything we will ever attempt." The walls of the conference room vibrate with screams of applause. "One thing I lack, however." The room falls silent, every eye locked onto the master. "I need more candy." Still silent, but respectful, the attendants wait to hear where "his badness" is heading with this.

"The best way to get the candy I need is to create a holiday. I'll call it Halloween, and I'll have all the dim-witted little rats run through neighborhoods dressed in ill-fitting Looney Tunes outfits, just after dark. They'll collect all the goodies I need from suckered homeowners." Screams of satisfaction! Once again, their leader has created a plan sure to captivate the attention of humankind. Not to mention all the tooth decay.

One daring demon raises his hand and carefully asks, "What about those putrid ... you know, the Christ-addicts? What if they retaliate?" The rest of the attendees hold their breath, scarcely believing their ears. The C.E.O. turns to face his questioner, slowly lowering his pointy chin. With one eyebrow raised, he replies: "It's alright if they come up with some moronic alternative to my plan. I'll just give them the idea of calling it Harvest Festival. I'll make sure they think it was their idea. It'll be the same thing, just different costumes. I'll still get the candy—and the distinct pleasure of watching little bodies convulsing with sugar highs."

●●●

Who really benefits from Halloween, anyway? The candy companies and dentists, that's about it. Parents don't benefit, they get hyper kids with rotting teeth. The neighborhoods don't benefit, they get unusable toilet paper and eggy windows. The stores don't benefit, either. There's always more candy for sale *after* the big event.

Even the kids don't benefit. When they're little they get scared by the older kids. When they're a bit older, they discover that they can get more candy when they *run* door to door. That's when they find out how impossible it is to see obstacles in their paths while squinting though small slits in a plastic Nixon mask (been there, with bruises). By the time they finally get old enough to be the ones doing the scaring, frightening little kids only gets them yelled at. What fun is that?

Halloween overflows with haunted houses, scary costumes, and the church-sponsored Hell House (also known as: "When Deacon Meetings Go Bad"). Halloween focuses on death, and this naturally plays into our fears about the "great unknown," something we all start moving toward as soon as we're born.

A typical conversation around the end of October will probably include some reference to scary stories or horror movies. So let me ask you: Why is it that the first person killed in horror movies is always the cheerleader? She turns unlimited back flips during every football game, but *must* seriously twist her ankle while running on flat ground trying to escape some loser wearing a hockey mask and seven sweaters.

But I digress. My point is: There are a great many notions regarding death, and *most of them are total misconceptions.* They seem to flow from our old childhood-induced "Halloween theology." But could we not think it through a little deeper? Whether the hellish board meeting ever took place or not, it appears the C.E.O. really has made some progress here.

Let's repair some of the damage. In this book, I want to explore with you the Christian perspective on death by asking, "What does death look like through the eyes of someone who personally knows Jesus?"

Recently I asked a friend, "What finally convinced you to open your life to Christ?" His answer surprised me. "After all my searching, I discovered that the Christian view of life and the after-life made the most sense," he said. "I used to live in fear of dying. But when I gave my life to Christ, I found a tremendous peace in knowing what to expect on the other side."

Do you know what to expect? Read on!

Chapter One

CAN DEATH DIE?

I started thinking deeply about the afterlife one day while driving home from a trip to Houston. You see, when I'm on a long trip, I often leave my radio on "seek," because I like listening to different kinds of music. Amazingly, while driving through Texas, I came across a country-western station! (Hey, one of the ways I can tell I need a rest stop is when I start singing along with country songs on the radio. I get teary eyed and start thinking about getting married. Time to pull off the road.) Anyway ... I was soon hearing these lyrics:

> *"If heaven ain't a lot like Texas,*
> *then I don't wanna go."*

I was already in Texas, so I figured I'd test out those lyrics by taking a good, hard look at the scenery. I'll admit the interstate isn't the best place to get the complete picture of the Lone Star state, but it's all I had to look at ... mile after fence-posted mile. My verdict? Well, imagine a steel guitar playing softly in the background, and I'll sing it for you:

"If heaven is a lot like Texas,
that would really stink."

Imagine living your whole life for Christ, dying and entering the afterlife, only to land in a place like Amarillo. What would that be like? You approach the Pearly Gate and notice that it has a mother-of-pearl inlaid cattle guard. Saint Peter stands there in a wife-beater shirt, leaning against the wall with a toothpick in the side of his mouth. He's got his dingy white robe cinched at the waist by a hand-tooled leather belt with a huge Dallas Cowboy Super Bowl XXX Championship buckle, and "PETE" stamped in the back. The keys to all the important places in heaven dangle ominously on his Elvis key chain.

His wings would be dusty from the dirt roads, his tattoo would say, "My boss is a Jewish Carpenter," and he'd be wearing a big trucker mesh hat with the imprint: "I'd rather be fishing." Once inside the gate, you'd immediately notice that all the mansions were doublewide trailers. One-ton duelies would be parked in every driveway, complete with sword racks in the rear windows and mud flaps picturing Yosemite Sam pointing his pistols at Satan and screaming, "Scram, varmint!" The tailgate logo says, "Lord 250 Diesel," and the horn plays the tune, "We Gotta Mighty Convoy."

Now get these images out of your mind. Heaven is *not* a lot like Texas. Yet most of us have such a pessimistic view of death that we live in mortal fear of it. Only when we see death from God's perspective will we be able to kill the fear of death and live in freedom.

The Bible offers a positive perception of the life after life. In 1 Timothy 6, the apostle Paul was beginning to show his age. Some might even say, he was circling the green. He had taken on a young mentor, Timothy, a minister at a small church that would one day grow into an eighty-five-thousand-member congregation. In the verses we'll study, Paul taught Timothy to keep eternity in view by making three choices. Are you ready to make those choices in your life too?

> " Only when we see death from God's perspective will we be able to kill the fear of death and live in freedom. "

Optimistically leaving can be good

Naturally, lots of people don't believe their death will be a good thing. That's understandable, because we don't know much about the afterlife. Here's what we *do* know: We know that one day we will die. Singer Dave Matthews said, "Death is the only thing in the future we've already done." Death is a guarantee, and so is meeting Christ face to face. We don't know *when* we're going to die or *how* we'll die. We just know that we are going to experience death.

The Bible makes it clear that a personal encounter with

Christ awaits everyone at the end of life. For nonbelievers, this is not the most pleasant thought. They might just as well say, "I think I'll opt out of that meeting. After some of the things I've done, it's just too personal." They envision a sword-wielding tyrant who sits on a large throne dispensing judgment.

For the believer, the thought of meeting Christ is just as ominous, but in quite different ways. When believers die, they break into the new world to meet the One who took on their sins, their scars, and their screw-ups. The picture of the afterlife changes completely when we see Christ as the One who died in our place, rather than an angry, sword-carrying judge. For us, Christ took upon himself the full measure of God's judgment. While it's true that he is our judge, he is a judge ruled by compassion.

> " Believers don't fear leaving this life; they are prepared for it. "

Can you imagine that first face-to-face meeting with your Savior? The welcoming embrace of Christ and the overwhelming sense of peace? This is the moment you've been waiting for! Being able to look forward to this moment brings freedom and hope to us believers. Expecting this meeting gives us the freedom to live life fearlessly. Instead of enduring under fear, we can live according to the great comfort of knowing that the One who sits on the throne of heaven constantly takes our side of things. He offers everything he has to make sure we live life to the fullest, here *and* there. So, believers don't fear leaving this life; they are prepared for it.

Oppose the lies of the grave

Death is so overwhelming to most people that they either make up lies, or believe others' lies, about what happens afterward. They've come to think they can just create the kind of afterlife they want. Most of the time, the imagery they choose leaves some moral "wiggle room"; thus it'll be easier to negotiate the final move in their favor. For these folks, the afterlife is like a cosmic board game, but they get to make up the rules as they play. Thus they're always guaranteed to win.

What are some of the common misconceptions about life afterlife? Here are the biggies:

Everybody gets in This is a popular false belief. Those who hold to it base their thinking on the truth that God is love: "So how could a God of love ever send anyone to hell?" They figure as soon as they die, they'll meet the Oak Ridge Boys singing, "Come on in, buddy, take your shoes off. Come on in, you did the best you could do. Come on in, take your choice of doublewides, and put out a jar-o-sun tea!" These people can't imagine that a God of love is also a God of justice, so they convince themselves that somehow everybody gets in.

You die, and it's over Recently I met a guy who believes that when you die, nothing happens. The lights go out, and your body returns to the ground. Not only is this unappealing, it naturally leads to a life whose chief end is the pursuit of pleasure, a frantic race to experience every possible enjoyment. "Soak up every available buzz," they say, "and ride every emotional high. After all, when it's over, that's all there is." It's a way of using death to justify a life in search of whatever gives pleasure. Talk about ultimate selfishness!

You get to do it all over again (and again and again) This is the idea of reincarnation. To me, it's like having to do the seventh grade all over again. Is this really something to look forward to? The idea that people get to come back as a bug or a fly or a frog is not only nonbiblical, it's far-fetched. If we are sentenced to continue through endless rounds of reincarnation until we learn the great cosmic lessons of life, maybe somebody should have at least published a syllabus first. One person told me she hoped to come back as a dog so she could lie around the house and eat all day. (Just her luck, she'll return as a bomb-sniffing dog. How's that for stress?)

> 66 Reincarnation. To me, it's like having to do the seventh grade all over again. 99

Good people go to heaven; bad people go to hell This false belief rides on a merit system of salvation. Here people think that if they can do a lot of good things, then the Almighty Tally Master (God) will count the good marks against the bad marks and let them into heaven. "If I can just do more good than bad, more humanitarian things than nonhumanitarian things, God's gonna have to unhook the velvet rope and say, 'Go for it.'" We all know that all good people get into heaven and all bad people go to hell, right?

> " The biblical view of life after life is that heaven is for sinners and hell is for good people. "

Wrong. How can anyone ever live up to the goodness-badness standards of any other person? And if we all get to make up our *own* list of good and bad, then why make up the list at all? If we get to change it anytime we want, then we might as well live any way we choose ... and make up the list just before we die (so it fits with our moral history).

Enough of the myths and misconceptions! The believer's view of the afterlife is quite different and grounds itself in God's Word. Both the origin and the end of life is Christ Jesus, "to Him be honor and eternal dominion!" (1 Tim. 6:16). The biblical view of life after life is that heaven is for sinners and hell is for good people. We know this is so, because of the way Jesus spoke about the people who get into heaven.

Whenever Jesus spoke about the people who entered heaven, it was always the outcast, the disenfranchised, the thieves, and the prostitutes. As Jesus himself put it: "I did not come to call the righteous, but sinners" (Matt. 9:13). These are the people who eventually came to the end of their rope and realized that they just couldn't live life without his life in their life. The people who get into heaven are those who realize they can't possibly do enough good things to justify their entrance. They come to a point of brokenness and say, "Jesus, you are my only hope."

On the cross, minutes before his death, Jesus turned to the thief being executed beside him and said, "Today you shall be with Me in Paradise" (Luke 23:43). Time was up for the thief. He had no time left to earn his way into heaven, but he met Jesus in paradise as a forgiven sinner. Zacchaeus was a tax collector who'd stolen far more money than he had taken legitimately for taxes. He admitted to Christ that he was a thief, and Jesus basically said, "This man has truly gotten it today, and he is now a member of My kingdom." Jesus met the woman at the well, who had been married to many different guys, and said to her, "If you will drink of this eternal water, you will live forever."

> " Hell swarms with people who were good, moral people but who were too proud to drop their front. "

This is why Jesus told his disciples they'd be amazed at who showed up in heaven. The last would be first and the first would be last. To us, Jesus would say those "last people" are the ones we overlook, figuring they'll never make it. But remember: Heaven is for sinners; hell is for "good" people.

Whenever Jesus talked about people going to hell, his words were always directed to the Pharisees, religious men who tried to live strictly by the rules. These were the church people of his day, the moral do-gooders. They had all the rules and the laws down pat and could toe the line better than anyone else. These people were so good at living life that they didn't need the life of Jesus in their life! They were very religious, but they were disconnected from Christ.

Jesus said that hell would be crowded with the proud, the arrogant, the self-sufficient. In their minds, God is for weak people who need a crutch. They are sufficient in their own right; they don't need Christ.

But about those who seem to show some humility? "I'm basically a decent person," they say. "I haven't done a lot of really bad things. I've been pretty moral, done some religious things, prayed some prayers, lit some candles. I even attended church at Christmas and Easter. I think God will be pleased with me." Such people have no real brokenness either. There is no point at which they came to the end of themselves and cried out in despair: "God, I can't do this life without you!"

Heaven is for sinners; heaven is for screw-ups; heaven is for people who realize they can't live life—or the life after—without the life of Christ. Hell swarms with people who were good, moral people but who were too proud to drop their front and in honest humility approach Christ in brokenness.

While we're in this life we must come to the point of honesty with ourselves and honesty with God. He invites us to drop our self-sufficiency in order to say, "It's not about being good, moral, toeing the line, or keeping the rules. It's about connecting my life with the life of Christ." This is the biblical view of the afterlife.

Open your life to God's life

Because life comes from Jesus, we're foolish to think we can experience genuine life apart from his life in us. Paul teaches this to his young apprentice, Timothy:

> *Fight the good fight of faith;* **take hold of the eternal life** *to which you were called, and you made the good confession in the presence of many witnesses. I charge you in the presence of God, who gives life to all things, and of Christ Jesus, who testified the good confession before Pontius Pilate, that you keep the commandment without stain or reproach until the appearing of our Lord Jesus Christ, which He will bring about at the proper time—He who is the blessed and only Sovereign, the King of kings and Lord of lords;* **who alone possesses immortality** *and dwells in unapproachable light, whom no man has seen or can see. To Him be honor and eternal dominion! Amen.*
>
> —1 Timothy 6:12–16 (emphasis added)

" Don't do it without Christ. "

Paul is basically telling Timothy, "As you live your life on this earth, don't do it without Christ. Don't try to do it

30

out of your own strength, cunning, or creativity. Instead, take a firm hold of the life of Christ, and you will discover everything real life has to offer.

"Who alone possesses immortality." The word *immortality* has a spooky feel to it. If you didn't grow up in church and Sunday school, you probably wouldn't want to be forced to stand up in class, spell the word, and use it in a sentence. It simply means "unable to die." Jesus alone is the single possessor of immortality. He will never *not* be alive. Jesus is both the Creator and all-sustainer of all life.

Since Jesus will not die, Paul instructs us to link our life with Christ's. In this way, Jesus' immortality becomes ours. Because he is the giver of life, and we are the receivers of his life, the character and qualities of his life become ours. This includes the quality of immortality. It is this quality of his life that enables us to live forever. When we link our lives to the life of Christ, asking him to step out of heaven and into our lives, we are given eternal (immortal) life. When we die, we leave this world and step into the presence of God.

The opposite of immortality, then, is "the ability to die." We are all born with this quality; it comes as standard equipment. There is nothing required of us to fulfill this part of our makeup.

A clear word about death is due at this point. Everyone dies; it's the natural end of living. Those who link their lives with Christ die physically, just as those who do not choose to link their lives with Christ. But immortality speaks of *life beyond death* in the same way that mortality speaks of *death beyond death.* Those who have the life of Christ die once. Those who do not have the life of Christ die twice—first when that final breath is exhaled, and again when they cross over into eternal disconnect from Christ.

Our world is full of technology, so let me see if I can use the well-known to identify the unknown. Death without the life of Christ is the final "Fatal Error"; the hard-drive crash with no hope of recovery; the permanent log off; the complete firewall failure; and the final ctrl, alt, del sequence. People who die without Christ are forever separated from the presence of God. You can call this disconnected, permanently switched off, broken off, or forever unconnected, but the result is the same. It is forever losing the ability to link up with the life of Christ.

This disconnection is the natural outcome of self-sufficiency, stubbornness, and pride. The individual who chooses to find life on his own voids his own warranty on life. God creates us all with the capacity for immortality, and Jesus' life, death, and resurrection guarantees that this capacity can be realized. But our preference for finding life *in ourselves* leads us to make our own alterations to the capacity we've been given. These self-directed modifications cancel the warranty God has placed on us through Jesus. We willfully choose to deny the Creator his rights to give us his life.

This is all very real and practical. When I was five years old, my dad left home and my mom had to work two jobs just to pay the bills. She sold real estate and coached a girls' field hockey team. She played both parental roles at home. Whenever I got in trouble, she would say, "You just wait until your father gets home!" Then she'd turn around and say, "I'm home!"

I didn't see my dad again until I was twenty-one. He didn't know much about my life history, didn't know about my experiences at school or about my future plans. He certainly had no idea I was going into the ministry. He lived his entire life trying to figure out life on his own, clearly disconnected from God.

> 66 Death without the life of Christ is the final 'Fatal Error'; the hard-drive crash with no hope of recovery ... 99

My dad drank and smoked cigarettes his whole life. He could finish off a case of Jack Daniels in a week. He chain-smoked five packs a day—on the same match!

He showed up my junior year of college when I carried eighteen hours and served as an intern pastor of a large church. One day I received a call that my dad had checked into a local hospital because parts of his body were beginning to shut down. The years of abuse were now catching up to him. The doctors could only make him comfortable; they couldn't stop the progression of death.

In between classes and my duties at church, I would travel to the hospital for visits with my dad. We were like two strangers trying to get to know each other. Sometimes

> **Why do people hang on so desperately to this world? Because their fears of the afterlife are so creepy.** ""

he was awake and we would talk. Other times he was asleep, and I just spent a few minutes looking at him, trying to understand as much of him as I could.

In the middle of finals, I found enough courage to talk with my dad about his life and Jesus. I told him how the life of Christ gives us eternal life, no matter what we've done in our past. I said that Jesus would remove all the sin accumulated by his search for life in himself.

I told my dad how Christ had gone to the cross for him, dying for all of his bad choices. I told him how he could link his life with the life of Christ and how Christ could be real in him. On that Thursday, my dad asked Jesus to step out of heaven and into his torn-up life. On Friday, he died.

I wish I had known my dad longer. I enjoyed the visits during those remaining days of his life.

They put my dad's body in a coffin, but he went to meet his Savior, face to face. My dad had transferred his full weight from himself and onto the life of Christ. He opened what was left of his life to the eternal life of Christ.

To the believer, death is not dark, scary, or gloomy. It's not a horrific event to be feared. It's not about haunted houses and goblins. At the same time, it is more than just the natural termination of life on earth. It is having *the promise of life completely fulfilled.* At death we break into the next life that is forever. We get new bodies (fat-free), and we take on a new existence.

Why do people hang on so desperately to this world? Because their fears of the afterlife are so creepy. If you are living in a state of fear, realize that death is the beginning of the fulfillment of all God created you to be. You can choose right now to kill the fear by linking your life with the life of Christ. Yes, death can die. It happens when you invite Jesus to step out of heaven and step into your heart. The beginning of life is the ending of death.

Chapter Two

WHAT'S ON THE BOTTOM OF JESUS' FEET?

We know we're going to die. We just don't want to think about it. When we do check out, there will be a funeral. Someone is going to come, stand over our casket, say a few words, and give us a first-class send off.

Amazing what gets said at funerals, though. I've heard people say things that—everybody knew—had more than one meaning:

"He loved life," which means: "Boy! Was he hyper-active!"

"He was gentle," which means: "What a wimp."

"Everybody loved her," which means: "She was a real jerk."

"We'll all miss her," which means: "Glad she's gone."

"He was generous," which means: "He was co-dependent and needy."

"He loved others," which means: "He was a predator."

"Family was important to her," which means: "She was never home."

My uncle was a mortician when I entered the ministry. He taught me how to tie a tie so I would look nice when I preached. To this day, I still have to lie down on my back to get the knot just right. I couldn't tie an acceptable double Windsor while standing up if my life depended on it.

> **Another thing I've wondered about is, 'Why do caskets have pillows?'**

During the past twelve years of ministry, I've preached my share of funerals, and there are a few things I still don't get about these gatherings. When people walk by the casket they always say the same thing: "Oh, doesn't he look natural?" That's the one thing dead people *don't* look like. When I see a body in a casket, I always think, "He looks dead to me."

Another thing I've wondered about is, "Why do caskets have pillows?" If you're not comfortable when they put your body in a box, that stain-covered piece of poly-filled cotton isn't going to make things any better. One of the first funerals I preached was my grandfather's. I spoke and then stood by the casket while everyone walked by to see how natural he looked. They buried him with his watch on. While everyone walked by, the presence of the watch caused me to wonder where Granddad was going, and why he had to be there on time. Was he late picking up his Lord 250 Diesel, or was something special happening on the north side of heaven?

And why are the biggest guys always chosen to carry the casket? Most caskets weigh about 200 to 300 pounds—and that's before you put one of their big buddies in it. These guys carry enough of their own mass going up and down stairs; do they really need to add another 100 pounds to the workout? And the poor guys that are on the downhill side!

The thing I understand least about death is this: Throughout our entire life we struggle to be on time, and one of the greatest obstacles to this is traffic lights. When we die, they put us in a hearse, and a motorcycle policeman stops all other traffic, letting us run all the stoplights on the way to the cemetery. It's the one occasion we don't need to be anywhere on time—and yet we get to run all the lights! It doesn't seem fair, does it? (Also, speaking of the motorcade, I'm still waiting to see a bumper sticker on a hearse that says, "I'd rather be living.")

When someone stands over the casket at the church or graveside and speaks final words over the body, the attendees leave, the casket goes into the ground, and men shovel dirt on top, covering it up. But that's not the end. For the believer, death is the beginning, the hyperlink to eternity. Because of what Jesus did to death, death is now nothing to be feared or anxiously anticipated. Jesus was executed, and then he was buried in a real tomb that was sealed with a boulder

> ❝ For the believer, death is the beginning, the hyperlink to eternity. ❞

> **Without the resurrection, we are hopelessly trapped in a life without meaning or purpose.**

weighing at least a ton. But his stay in the grave was short, just three days. Then he rose from the dead. This one event is the point upon which all of Christianity balances.

The center of the Christian faith is the resurrection of Jesus Christ. It all rises and falls on Jesus coming back to life. If he did not rise from the dead, then ...

Christianity is a lie;
ministry is pointless;
morality doesn't matter;
life is futile;
suffering is senseless;
and reality is absurd.

Without the resurrection, we are hopelessly trapped in a life without meaning or purpose. But Jesus *did* rise from the dead, and his resurrection triggered a series of five events that change lives to this very day.

The apostle Paul pens the foundational truth on the subject of the resurrection in 1 Corinthians 15. He is writing to a group of believers who have had a great deal of false teaching presented to them regarding the resurrection. Twenty years after Jesus had left the earth, Paul writes to explain how Christ's rising from death changes everything. In just a few brief verses, he explains how the resurrection affected him and how it can permanently affect their lives too. For all of us, the resurrection can forever change the way we look at life and death. What, exactly, did it do?

It settled the cosmic rumble

He has abolished all rule and all authority and power.

—1 Corinthians 15:24

Inside heaven, long before the world was created, Lucifer and the angels he recruited launched a mutiny intent on replacing God's will and power with Lucifer's will and power. The insurrection failed, and the rebels were pushed out of heaven into the cosmos. In this act of permanent separation, death was born.

The mutineers were forced to live outside of heaven, and the world they made for themselves was darkness, chaos, and void. The realm they constructed was not a province of life, but a region of death, of eternal separation from God. Before the insurrection, there was no death; eternal separation only became possible through Lucifer's choices and actions.

His domain exists because of his obsession with de-creating anything God created, including our world. In one sense, Lucifer holds a title to the world: "the whole world lies in the power of the evil one" (1 John 5:19). Satan, then, was the lawful owner of the cosmos. His activities fill history and come through in the pages of the Bible. Why do the Scriptures record Lucifer's de-creation story? Because it provides the perfect backdrop for God's compassionate activities of redemption.

In Scripture, everything God did was for the purpose of redeeming creation and removing forever the source of evil. He spoke through the prophets because of his plan. His plan called for Jesus to come to the earth. And his plan involves the church—the reason the church is still relevant for the world today.

The arrival of Jesus into the cosmic scene is God's announcement to Lucifer and humankind that the Almighty King has come to redeem the world and, once and for all, reclaim legal hold over his creation. The death of Jesus on the cross provides Lucifer with one final moment of false victory. Three days later, Jesus, who had been laid in the tomb, rose from the dead. The resurrection broke any legal hold Lucifer held on the cosmos and reclaimed ownership for God. The resurrection removed the tyrannical leader and restored ultimate and final authority to God, the compassionate Creator of the cosmos.

> "Death occurs on many levels, and the resurrection of Jesus impacts them all."

Death occurs on many levels, and the resurrection of Jesus impacts them all. On a cosmic level, Jesus' resurrection reclaimed everything that was at stake. His resurrection guaranteed God's redemption of everything he had created. By his resurrection, Jesus defeated death, toppling the tyrant and crushing his authority.

Lucifer's authority has been broken, but the world can still feel the effects of his power. As long as Lucifer held legal hold over the world, God's agenda was the competing agenda. But after the resurrection of Jesus, the question as to whose will and power would remain in control was once and for all settled. God now has the last word.

It seated Christ as regent

He has put all things in subjection under His feet.
—1 Corinthians 15:27

When Jesus entered heaven, the Father seated him at his right hand. As Jesus took his place there, God declared that all things were subject to Jesus—the entire cosmos, all of humankind and creation, and all of his enemies. This verse echoes phrases in Psalm 110:1–2, "until I make Your enemies a footstool for Your feet ... rule in the midst of Your enemies." In Bible days, the conquering king would often make the defeated ruler lie down in front of his throne so he could use the poor guy's neck as an ottoman. Here Jesus himself sits on his throne with the neck of his enemies as his footstool. He was seated in heaven as the regent over everything. A regent is a person governing for a sovereign. Jesus represents God's rule throughout all creation.

After his resurrection, Jesus spent several more weeks on the earth before returning to heaven. As he left the earth, he

> ❝ In our own power, we cannot undo the effects of darkness, nor can we make the darkness submit to us. ❞

reminded his disciples who witnessed his ascension that "all authority has been given to Me in heaven and on earth" (Matt. 28:18). They needed to remember that what he had won through his resurrection he now carried with him back to heaven. He was not leaving his winnings on the table; they were his permanent possession and were with him wherever he went. As the disciples watched Jesus leave the earth, they knew that the authority for living life resided in the living, risen Christ.

We live in an imperfect world. Jesus reigns as the ultimate regent over the cosmos, but we must still endure ongoing attempts at de-creation by Lucifer, the defeated tyrant. Christ is in control, and the government of darkness has been reduced to a minority status. Our authority for living resides not in ourselves but in the person of Christ, who is forever seated at the right hand of God. In our own power, we cannot undo the effects of darkness, nor can we make the darkness submit to us. Thankfully, through his resurrection Jesus has already done all of this on our behalf. In him we can find the peace and power to operate freely in this imperfect world.

It sabotaged the rebellion

"O DEATH, WHERE IS YOUR VICTORY? O DEATH, WHERE IS YOUR STING?"

—1 Corinthians 15:55

God devised a plan to remove the effects of Lucifer's rebellion, once and for all. He initiated his plan in Genesis 1:1 by creating the earth, which was to become ground zero for ending all evil and rebellion.

God created the Garden of Eden perfect and separate from the chaos of the cosmos, so there was no cosmic rumble within it. The earth and everything in it was God's creation. He held the title; it was his legal possession. He placed Adam and Eve in the world to tend it and to be fruitful and populate it.

But then Lucifer appeared in the form of a serpent and tempted Eve to do as he himself had done: choose her own competing plan against God's established eternal plan. After she made her own choice, Adam made his own choice with the same result. Lucifer had

> " All humans are born dead. They have a pulse, they breath air, they move and speak, but they are born into an existence for which they were never created: the deadness of moral and spiritual separation from God. "

45

accomplished his purpose of deception, tricking humans into handing over the freedom and life that God had given them. Humankind was now indebted by sin; Satan held deed to their lives.

> " Their choices had enabled evil to enter the perfect creation of God. "

The choices Adam and Eve made allowed the rumble between Lucifer and God to trespass into the perfect creation of the world. They were de-created from what God had created them to be. And everyone born after that time takes first breath in that de-created state. That is, all humans are born dead. They have a pulse, they breathe air, they move and speak, but they are born into an existence for which they were never created: the deadness of moral and spiritual separation from God. Sadly, this is the unavoidable birthright of every human being ever born.

On the evening of the day Adam and Eve chose their own agenda, God came for his daily walk with them. When they heard God approaching, they hid themselves in the bushes because they sensed a separation between themselves and God for the first time in their lives. They knew they'd done something that had fundamentally damaged the relationship.

They had eaten the fruit of the tree of knowledge and were therefore expelled from the garden. Their choices had enabled evil to enter the perfect creation of God. God posted an angel at the entrance to the garden to prevent Adam and Eve from returning and eating from the tree of everlasting life.

All of this is the sad story of the rebellion. But the good news is that, through his resurrection, Jesus did something for us that we could never do for ourselves: He sabotaged the rebellion. His resurrection makes it possible for every person to be re-created into the creation God designed humankind to be. In order for this to happen, human beings must pass from death to life. Jesus' resurrection makes this possible.

Lucifer planned to hold all of humankind as his possession forever. He knew how much God loved the world and how much he loved all of his creation, including humanity. He knew that the only way he could ever de-create the entire world was to gain ownership of that part of cre-

> **"We've done more finger-pointing than a fat guy in a donut shop."**

ation created in God's own image ... man and woman.

We are just like Adam and Eve in that we are our own worst enemy. We choose to advance our own agenda and then try to blame everything but ourselves. We've done more finger-pointing than a fat guy in a donut shop. Were it not for the resurrection of Jesus, we would forever remain the property of Satan. Were it not for the resurrection of

Jesus, the process of de-creation would never have been defeated.

It secured our reputation

We will also bear the image of the heavenly.

—1 Corinthians 15:49

66 Jesus permanently fills the right-hand position of God; we are already in him, and he is going nowhere. 99

When anyone asks Jesus to step out of heaven and step into her heart, something more happens than most believers realize. The Scripture teaches in Romans 6:3–5 that a metamorphosis takes place unlike any other in life.

Or do you not know that all of us who have been baptized into Christ Jesus have been baptized into His death?

Therefore we have been buried with Him through baptism into death, so that as Christ was raised from the dead through the glory of the Father, so we too might walk in newness of life. For if we have become united with Him in the likeness of His death, certainly we shall also be in the likeness of His resurrection.

These verses describe the way our position in eternity is absorbed in the completed activities of Jesus Christ when he was crucified, buried, and raised from the dead. Because we are already in Christ, when he left this earth and ascended to the right hand of God we, in effect, went with Him. We already have our heavenly position sealed because he securely holds his position as the Regent of Creation. We do not need to be concerned that heaven will become over-crowded—our position is secured in Him. We do not need to worry that our position will become compromised. Jesus permanently fills the right-hand position of God; we are already in him, and he is going nowhere.

The resurrection has more than a *future* effect. It also impacts our everyday lives here on the earth. New Testament believers recognized baptism as representing a turning point in their lives. They knew that their lives cohabited with Christ and that everything about them was different. They were still humans, but now their lives bore the authentic image of Christ. They were well acquainted with the sins of their lives, but they recognized that they were no longer required to bear the responsibility for sin's pun-ishment. Christ had already taken their punishment.

> " Death misunderstood leads to life misdirected. "

They recognized that their lives would be different, too. They would think differently, act differently, and make choices differently. They knew that because of their posi-tion in Christ their lives would carry a weight they could never have carried before. The impact of their lives would now have eternal impact.

The power that God released to defeat death and bring Jesus back to life was present in the days Jesus appeared to people *after* his resurrection. That same power is present in the life of every believer. The resurrection of Christ nearly 2,000 years ago makes a permanent mark on the present tense life of the believer. Our lives are linked, identified, branded, welded, and fused with Christ's. The way we look at life changes. The way we approach our problems is different. We learn how to turn our reactions into responses, and our responses become more and more like his. The resurrection of Christ changes the way we take on life and death.

It supercharged our relationship

> *Your toil is not in vain in the Lord.*
> —1 Corinthians 15:58

Many people tell me they live for the moment because the future offers nothing better than what they can experience *right now.* They live for the pleasure of the moment, the maximum thrill, the quick fix, and the search for the next new shiny thing that promises something they haven't tried.

For them, death is like the "Game Over" graphic when a video character runs out of lives. They make silly remarks about death, trying to distance themselves from the one thing that will put an end to pleasure seeking. They both fear death and embrace it, for this is the place from which their despair for life originates.

But we all need to realize that death misunderstood leads to life misdirected. Only the believer is truly capable of grasping the meaning of death and thereby the purpose and direction of life.

The connection every believer has with the life, death, burial, and resurrection of Christ makes it possible to bring to bear in our own lives every resource Christ had in his life here on earth. In other words, for every situation we face, the unlimited wisdom and power

> " Jesus' life moved them to change the way they lived, but his resurrection empowered them to live the changed life. "

of Christ waits to be applied. Everything he carried with him while on the earth, we carry with us every day, because we carry him in his fullness inside us.

There is no trouble so fearful that his peace cannot settle. There is no pain so great that his comfort cannot heal. There is no lack so severe that his resources cannot accommodate. There is no emptiness so vast that his companionship cannot fill.

Jesus experienced loneliness, hunger, pain, separation, exhaustion, intimidation, fear, and the loss of loved ones. All of the things we experience and feel, he felt and experienced before us. And everything we need to face any situation is available in our relationship with him. Jesus understands life; he lived it. Jesus understands physical pain; he endured it. He understands the emotional destruction rejection brings; he lived with it every day. He completely identifies with the permanency of death; he grew close to many while on the earth and saw many of them die.

Whatever we face, the resurrection of Christ provides us with the unmistakable knowledge that he is forever with us, never leaving us. He helps us see as he saw, and he provides his perspective on the situations of life. The struggles of life don't have to wear us down, because we have the never-ending resurrected life of Christ living in us. It can carry us through anything, supercharged and coming out on top.

The disciples who spent just over three years with Jesus while he was here on earth were moved and touched by the things they saw him do. But it was the resurrection that changed their lives. While he was with them, they watched as he did the ministry, touching people and healing the sick. But when he was crucified, they experienced the loss of their hope for life. The three days Jesus spent in the tomb were the longest the disciples had ever lived. They were left with their memories of him, with the stories they could tell, with the laughter of shared experiences, and the with somber lessons of life he taught through parables of wheat grains, foolish builders, and compassionate fathers.

Jesus' life moved them to change the way they lived, but his resurrection empowered them to live the changed life. The tax collector became the writer of the first Gospel,

Matthew. The loud ones, James and John, became pastors of two of the first churches to see thousands accept Christ. Peter, who denied him, became so outspoken for Christ that he was ultimately sentenced to die by crucifixion. But this once fearful man requested that he be executed upside down, feeling unworthy to die as Jesus died.

Many of us are touched and moved by the stories of Jesus—his birth, the miracles he performed, the stories he told, and the death he suffered. But nothing changes a life like the resurrection of Christ when it becomes a living reality to the believer. Life takes on new meaning, duties acquire new purpose, and death no longer scares us. Death is now understood—because of what Jesus did to it.

Chapter Three

What happens sixty seconds after I die?

What happens at the moment of death remains a mystery for us all. We can prepare for its coming—even anticipate it—but still remain in fear of it. We wonder whether our death will be sudden, as in a fatal car crash, or more drawn out, as with a long-term illness.

What we really wonder about is what happens *after* death. Will I get lost between here and the gates of heaven? Will my name be recorded, or will a minimum-wage celestial clerk mistakenly erase *my* name instead of the Satan-worshiping warlock David Edwards, who lived in the late 1600s?

We don't think too much about what happens to other people; we just assume that their reservations for flight and accommodations will all turn out okay. But will ours? And when we get there, what can we expect? Will we know anyone, or will we wander the golden streets with a nametag, hoping somebody will make an introduction or two.

Perhaps there will be icebreakers in heaven—you know, a time when we all get together, meet the heroes of

Scripture, and share what life was like for us, pre-heaven. I imagine heaven's processing center for registration and orientation. The newcomers for that day are ushered into a large hall, where hundreds of chairs await them in circles of six to eight.

> **Perhaps there will be icebreakers in heaven—you know, a time when we all get together, meet the heroes of Scripture, and share what life was like for us, pre-heaven.**

While looking for an empty seat, a lady wanders over to a circle and listens in for a moment. Here's Mary (the one who poured oil over Jesus' feet) telling her story: "I took the most valuable thing I had. That perfume was worth almost a full year's wages. I broke it and poured it over his feet, and then I dried his feet with my hair. I gave what I had." That's when the listening lady decides to jump into the sharing: "Yea, I know what you mean. I gave two cans of hominy grits to the local food drive. I'm with you on the sacrificial giving thing, sister!"

The next circle features Old Testament hero Noah: "Well, as you probably already know, I built a large boat, and brought on board two of every kind of animal. Then I collected enough food for all the animals and my family. It rained for forty days and forty nights without letting up." One guy in the circle speaks up and says, "Been there with the heavy rain, Noh-bro. My buddy and I went through the same thing when we were at the OU vs. Baylor game. We'd had a little bit too much to drink, and it poured rain the whole first half." Noah smiles kindly before adding, "After the flood waters receded, I went outside and worshiped God under the very first rainbow. That was God's promise never to destroy the earth by water again." The gal sitting beside Noah timidly says, "Just before I got here, I was wearing a toga, a rainbow of beads, and a feather boa. I still don't know how I fell off that float."

Suppose you're walking around observing all these interactions. The next circle is full, but you can't help listening in as Moses speaks: "God called me to lead millions of people out of Egypt and into the Promised Land. They were a stubborn people, and God made us wander around the desert for forty years. But he fed us manna and quail until we reached the land he had promised." Then a young college student chimes in: "I hate eating the same thing all the time. I remember one week when I only had four dollars for food and had to survive on Ramen noodles with that little seasoning pack." The circle of heads nod, all except Moses, whose eyes widen just a bit as he struggles to understand the connection. A young female coed then shares her frustrating experience of wandering: "My girlfriends and I were at the mall, you know, and like, wouldn't remember where we parked Daddy's Beemer, you know, and we like wandered around the parking lot for like an hour before we found it. And, like, it was right

> **"C'mon you all, it's not that bad. I once swallowed a goldfish."**

where we parked it. How weird is that?"

There's an empty seat in the next circle, but you decide to listen in a bit before joining the group. John the Baptist is heaven's diplomat of this circle, and he's already fielding questions. "I hear you used to eat locusts" one man asks. "That's right," John replies. "Once roasted, they're actually quite tasty, kind of like deep-friend cheese sticks." The guy's face seems to say: *Overshare!* But an older man chuckles and adds: "C'mon you all, it's not that bad. I once swallowed a goldfish."

The depth of that conversation has you quickly moving to eavesdrop on the next circle, where Daniel is sharing his story of persecution for his faith. "Simply because I remained faithful and prayed, I was thrown into a pit of hungry lions." Some in the circle had thought this story was only a fable from the Bible. Now they sit slack-jawed and speechless. One young red-headed hyperactive boy keeps swinging his feet under the chair while saying: "My mom and dad punished me one time, and took away all my videos except *The Lion King*. It was the only movie I got to watch for three whole days!"

Finally, you find your own circle near the back of the room. There are three empty seats—and very quickly you discover why: The apostle Paul is leading the discussions here. Sitting there with him will be intimidating, but you decide to give it a try. As you take your seat, Paul reminds the group, "I took three really long mission trips. I endured stoning and shipwreck for the cause of Christ. I built the church, and I wrote half of the New Testament." You're the newcomer to the group, so Paul looks your way, motions with his hand, and encourages you with a silent nod to share your story. Your mind races to find something of significance to say. Your lips begin to move, and you can scarcely believe the words coming out of your mouth. "Does everyone remember that little book, the *Prayer of Jabez?* Well, I read half of it. I didn't make it all the way through, because I got so sleepy."

> "Death is actually a thin shell around the mortal portion of our life that must be broken if we're to experience eternity."

Okay, maybe you won't step into icebreaker sharing as soon as you enter heaven. We just don't know.

But here's something we do know: Death happens in an instant. It's the piercing of a veil as thin as a piece of tracing paper. Death is actually a thin shell around the mortal portion of our life that must be broken if we're to experience eternity. On one side of this veneer is life as we know it; on the other side is eternity—that for which we were created.

On the whole, the Bible isn't negative or morbid when

it deals with the subject of death. Rather, it's positive—especially when it addresses the death of a believer. The more we understand the chain of events initiated by death, the more we'll be able to see the prospect of death as a positive rather than a negative influence on our life and actions. The Bible highlights five sequential events initiated when death arrives for us:

Removed from this dimension

> ... to be absent from the body and to be at home with the Lord.
>
> —2 Corinthians 5:8

Death is not so much the ending of life as it is the switching of dimensions. Think about it in terms of being born, for example. Birth ushers us into a new dimension of life, one previously undiscovered. The human baby rests inside its mother for nine months, where it is continuously fed through

> " When we die, we go directly into his presence. "

the umbilical cord. It fills its lungs with the fluid from the embryonic sac and actually responds to outside stimuli.

But once born, the baby's consistent source of nourishment is cut, and it is forced to get the oxygen it needs by filling its lungs with air. Inside its mother, the baby was completely alive, and even though it could not see or smell, its experience of life was nonetheless real. Once outside its mother, the baby's experience of life is quite different—but it is the exact environment for which the baby was born. We might say that a healthy birth is a "victory" for all concerned, parents and child.

There is victory in death. The moment we die, we immediately go to be with God. Our spirit doesn't languish in some cosmic cryogenic lab, waiting to meet Christ. When we die, we go directly into his presence.

Receive a new design

... who will transform the body of our humble state into conformity with the body of His glory.

—Philippians 3:21

Take a walk in any big shopping mall, and you'll quickly be reminded that our bodies wear out. I'm talking about the walkers' clubs. Every mall has them: senior citizens in sweatsuits and gym shoes, some of them carrying little weights in their hands, moving quickly through the crowds with looks of intense concentration. I *will* stay young!

66 Our bodies are temporary; they die. They were created as the earthly vessels for our life; they were not created for eternal life in heaven. 99

These folks are trying to slow down the natural deterioration process that overcomes all physical bodies. Try as they might, they can't avoid that slow but inevitable decline. Their joints will finally wear out, their eyesight will dim, and their muscles will one day refuse to carry them from the Gap to Cinnabons.

Our bodies are temporary; they die. They were created as the earthly vessels for our life; they were not created for eternal life in heaven. Heaven is the eternal city, so only the timeless reside there. The temporary cannot enter the domain of the timeless; therefore, at death we leave behind the temporary body.

We take on a timeless body. The Bible doesn't give us many details about the redesigned body, but it does tell us a few things that will help us make sense of what happens to us after death. For example, we know that our timeless body will be unique in its appearance and be easily recognizable. And the type of body we'll have is the same type as Jesus had after his resurrection.

> **The type of body we'll have is the same type as Jesus had after his resurrection.**

Recall how that body worked. Several days after his death, Jesus' disciples sat in a home behind locked doors, discussing what they should do now that Jesus was no longer with them. Suddenly Jesus appeared to them:

Then He said to Thomas, "Reach here with your finger, and see My hands; and reach here your hand and put it into My side; and do not be unbelieving, but believing."

—John 20:27

66 For the first time, we will see ourselves as we truly are. 99

With his redesigned body, Jesus was able to appear and then disappear before their eyes. This is the type of body we will have once we're redesigned.

Several days later, the disciples were fishing from a boat when Peter recognized Jesus on the shore cooking some fish. Peter immediately dove into the water and swam to the beach. The rest of the disciples rowed the boat to shore to join Peter and Jesus. During this encounter Jesus cooked fish, broke bread, and spoke to them audibly. The disciples recognized Jesus, touched Him, spoke with him, and afterward knew they'd encountered the same Jesus with whom they had spent three years of their lives. They must have thought the redesign was a good thing.

Revealing our decisions

For now we see in a mirror dimly, but then face to face; now I know in part, but then I will know fully just as I also have been fully known.

—1 Corinthians 13:12

The dimensional switch that takes place at death is instantaneous and irreversible, the chain of events being unavoidable. And each step of the way, we are active participants in

> **He is our Savior and our judge; he sees every explicit detail of our true selves. And then, without any hidden agenda, he offers us his life.**

the process. One instant we're on the earth; the next, we're with Jesus. Before death we trudged around in a temporary body; after death, we receive a timeless body. And then each of us will proceed to the defining moment of clarity.

All believers will stand before Christ and face the most precise accounting of their life: their actions, their thoughts, their motives, and their decisions. We have never known any experience like this, in which the explicit details of our lives become completely visible between Jesus and us. Normally, we can wrap ourselves in layers of justification and rhetoric, but "escape tactics" become immediately transparent. For the first time, we will see ourselves as we truly are.

We will also see Jesus as he truly is: our judge. The veneer we created to manipulate people's opinions about us becomes see-through to the judge. For the first time, we become fully aware of what he has known all along. He is our Savior and our judge; he sees every explicit detail of our true selves. And then, without any hidden agenda, he offers us his life.

We will see what our lives *could have* become. We'll realize the impact our decisions had on our entire history. This will most obviously not be a typical awards ceremony for any of us. Our life is going to be judged, and we will have to look squarely at our degree of faithfulness to what we were given.

I speak with many people who are excited about heaven, because they've assumed that when they show up, the fun-loving cast of heaven's re-creation of "What Not to Wear" will meet them and take them shopping for their new body. They figure the redesigning process takes about as long as it does to pick up a white robe and get a quick make-over.

The process is actually more like what happens on "American Idol." Thousands show up and register for a preliminary audition. They get their number tags and pin it to their shirts, and then wait their turn to sing for a trio of judges. Each contestant has prepared and feels completely ready for this moment. Simon, Paula, and Randy sit behind their table, pencils ready. A smile from Paula lets the contestant know that it's time to show them the best he has to offer.

Ten seconds into the audition, Randy gets up and walks out, Paula hides her face. Simon shuts his eyes and slowly shakes his head, hardly believing the horrific sounds which, the contestant had assured them, was "a song." Simon holds up his hand and the contestant stops singing. Anxious for Simon's approval, the contestant drops two bullets of sweat from his underarm. Simon speaks: "That was ... *horrible*. I've heard bad and worse, but you are worse than worse."

A moment of profound clarity begins to show on the

guy's face. Never before has anyone been so blatantly honest about his performance, the best he had to offer.

When we stand before Christ, everything about our lives will be brought into account. Everything left undone that God had planned for us to do will be measured against the things we chose to do instead. The results of our decisions will become the evidence of our need for Jesus.

Rewards are distributed

For no man can lay a foundation other than the one which is laid, which is Jesus Christ.

Now if any man builds upon the foundation with gold, silver, precious stones, wood, hay, straw, each man's work will become evident; for the day will show it because it is to be revealed with fire, and the fire itself will test the quality of each man's work. If any man's work which he has built on it remains, he will receive a reward. If any man's work is burned up, he will suffer loss; but he himself shall be saved, yet so as through fire.

—1 Corinthians 3:11–15

66 **Did we maximize our opportunities or bail on them when things got tough?** 99

Everything we have done after Jesus came to inhabit our lives will be put to the test, based on our fidelity to the things of God. We have all experienced infidelity in some way in our lives. We have made and lost friends who didn't stay faithful, and we have each looked into the mirror only to see someone whose fidelity to personal integrity has often been compromised.

The foundation for life is Jesus Christ, and we have the opportunity to live in fidelity to his purposes and plans. We also have the freedom to live any other way we choose. But how we use our time will be put to the test. What is our measure of fidelity when our use of time is measured by the standard of Christ? The way we use our money will also be graphed beside the standards of Christ. What we did with the talents, abilities, and opportunities placed before us will also be tested. Did we maximize our opportunities or bail on them when things got tough? Did we develop our talents and abilities into something that expanded the kingdom?

Everything about our lives will be put to the test. The things we did merely to build our own legacy will fail the test. Only those things we built on the foundation of Christ will pass. And for those Spirit-empowered works, Jesus will award us crowns.

The rewards, or crowns, believers receive have been a subject of debate for centuries. What they are exactly, no one knows for certain. A friend of mine has a young son who, like most children, loves to color in coloring books. He uses his big box of sixty-four crayons to create his refrigerator masterpieces. My friend likes to sit and color with his son and share the crayons, but the little boy asks for the red "crown" or the blue "crown" instead of saying *crayon*. How disappointing would it be to live a life of fidelity with the things of Christ, only to discover (from those receiving their reward before you) that Jesus was handing out crayons? And what would it mean if you got the one labeled "Burnt Sienna"?

In any case, I'm quite sure the crowns are not literal pieces of gold encrusted with jewels to be worn on our heads. They are Jesus' way of confirming approval on the things we have done. They are his ultimate kudos, given in recognition of our fidelity to Him. Let's look them over:

The crown of reliability "Everyone who competes in the games exercises self-control in all things" (1 Cor. 9:25). This crown recognizes those believers who brought their impulses under control. They demonstrated appreciable degrees of self-control in all areas of life, but not because they wanted to gain position or power or approval by others. Rather, they wanted to deepen their qualifications to build on the foundation Christ had already laid in their lives.

The crown of rejoicing "For who is our hope or joy or crown of exultation? Is it not even you, in the presence of our Lord Jesus at His coming?" (1 Thess. 2:19).

Paul referred to the churches he had established—and the people who had come to Christ through his ministry—as his crown of rejoicing. The foundation of Christ is the building and expanding of his kingdom throughout the world. The people impacted by our lives, those whom we personally led to Christ, and those positively influenced by the ripples of our ministry ... these are our own crown of rejoicing.

The crown of righteousness "In the future there is laid up for me the crown of righteousness, which the Lord, the righteous Judge, will award to me on that day; and not only to me, but also to all who have loved His appearing" (2 Tim. 4:8).

Paul exemplified fidelity with Christ. He faced everything in life with faith and trust in the Lord he had personally come to know through the tough times in life. He waited anxiously to receive his Master's recognition for the way he had lived. Paul had made the hard choices, taking whatever steps necessary to keep his life always ready to make an impact for the kingdom. This is practical, daily righteousness demonstrated in the life of any believer who chooses to be constantly ready to advance Christ's kingdom. This believer will receive the same recognition as Paul.

The crown of resolution "Do not fear what you are about to suffer. Behold, the devil is about to cast some of you into prison, so that you will be tested, and you will have tribulation for ten days. Be faithful until death, and I will give you the crown of life" (Rev. 2:10).

This is the Lifetime Fidelity Award given to those who remain resolute in faith, regardless of the type or intensity of the opposition they face. It is special recognition given by Jesus to those who suffer physical persecution and death at the hands of those who seek to destroy the works of Christ on the earth.

> ❝It's for parents who put Jesus' fame before the obedience and respect they expected from the kids. It's for bosses who put Christ's fame ahead of the loyalty they expected from their employees, and employees who did the same thing in their relationship with their bosses.❞

The crown of renown

"And when the Chief Shepherd appears, you will receive the unfading crown of glory" (1 Peter 5:4).

This crown goes to believers who placed the fame of Jesus way out in front of their own. It's for parents who put Jesus' fame before the obedience and respect they expected from the kids. It's for bosses who put Christ's fame ahead of the loyalty they expected from their employees, and employees who did the same thing in their relationship with their bosses. They chose to value the fame of Christ in their friendships more than they valued the latest juicy gossip.

The crowns symbolize Jesus' recognition of our cooperation with his plans for worldwide redemption. They are given according to his perfect judgment, not our individual merit. We will not stand around in heaven comparing crowns, either. It will be immaterial if you have three, and the person standing next to you has only one. We will not have audience voting pads in the back of chairs that allow us to vote on whether or not somebody deserves two or four crowns. We will simply celebrate with everyone else at the recognition Jesus gives for the work we have done.

Finally, the Scripture says we'll return our crowns to Jesus in a huge worship event. (I truly hope that what we lay down at Jesus' feet are crowns. I'd be embarrassed to lay down an "Autumn Sunset Orange.")

Rank is determined

Jesus tells a parable about a wealthy man who went on a long journey. The man called three of his servants and gave them money to invest while he was gone. To one he gave 50 percent of his money, to another he gave 20 percent, and to the third he gave 10 percent. (The man kept the other 20 percent for another parable ... but I digress.)

The man was gone for several years. During that time, the servant entrusted with 50 percent earned an equal amount of money and presented it to his master when he returned. The servant in charge of 20 percent returned another 20 percent back to his master. But the servant with 10 percent to watch over returned exactly the same money his master had given him.

The first two servants received praise—and more responsibility, because they had proven themselves faithful in the little things. But the servant who did nothing except bury his master's money in the ground was punished for his choice. The 10 percent was taken from him and given to the servant

> 66 Our dependability on earth determines our responsibility in heaven. 99

who had doubled the master's 50 percent.

Many of us have been taught that what we do here on earth has little or nothing to do with our position in heaven. We have been taught that heaven is an egalitarian state where no one carries more influence than any one else. The Scripture doesn't bear this out. Jesus is telling us: Our dependability on earth determines our responsibility in heaven. Everyone who receives Christ Jesus gets to go to heaven, but not everyone receives the same role or position.

Here's another example: Jesus and his disciples were walking along one day when an argument broke out. The disciples were hassling about who would be the greatest in the kingdom. Jesus responded, "The first will be last and the last the first." Doesn't Jesus indicate by that statement the possibility of varying roles and ranks in heaven?

Perhaps now the moment that immediately follows death is not such a mystery. For the believer, death is nothing to be feared. For the nonbeliever, I hope this material has helped you see more clearly your need for Christ.

The moment we are born, the fuse leading to this chain of events flares into flame. Death serves as the blasting cap putting into motion this wonderful sequence. These things happen in rapid-fire fashion. It's not as if you're in line at the

DMV to get your license renewed. It all takes place in a matter of moments.

In the first sixty seconds of eternity, each believer experiences an amazing array of adventures. There is nothing to fear, because heaven is the place we were created to inherit. The way we die is of no consequence to the way we spend eternity; however, the way we *live* does have eternal consequences.

Chapter Four

HOW WILL I KNOW IF I'M DEAD?

Maybe we'll all die of old age at 104. And with any luck, we won't die in an embarrassing way, like ...

- overdosing on Rogaine;
- mooning from the back of a speeding pickup—and falling out;
- exploding in a pie-eating contest;
- drowning in a cereal bowl after taking too many shots of nighttime NyQuil;
- being shot to death by a salad shooter (there was a carrot in the chamber, and he never saw it coming).

Being hit by an ice-cream truck would be embarrassing, and quite sad. The last thing you would hear is that crazy, out-of-tune music fading, and a dozen kids screaming ... as they chased after the truck. Or how about bleeding to death from a safety-scissors injury? Or suffocating in the ball pit at Chuck-E-Cheese?

> **"The Bible is fairly clear on the type of life container we will have in heaven."**

No self-respecting outdoorsman would want to die in a hunting accident, falling asleep in a tree-top deer stand, only to tumble thirty-six feet to the forest floor and then be shot by his own gun. Talk about expiration embarrassment! But I've known a few people who have actually used a blow dryer while taking a shower. I saw one guy choke to death on Jell-O, and heard about another who overdosed on suppositories.

Countless university students have died while attempting to break this dubious record: who can hold the most marshmallows in his mouth? Thousands of people die every year snorting Sweet-n-Low to get high—or die of unknown causes, seven days after watching *The Ring*. But I don't know anyone who would want to die falling off the float in Mardi Gras, wearing feathers and beads.

None of us knows *how* we're going to die, and most of us don't want to know *when* we're going to die. If we knew these two things, Death would be robbed of the only pleasure he gets from his job: the element of surprise. The Bible is fairly clear on the type of life container we will have in heaven. Here on earth, we call it a body. In heaven it will be something similar, but quite different. The Bible surely uses the word "body" when talking about our spiritual life container as a reference point for our mortal understanding. The actual scope and construct of this afterlife body is unknown.

We are not the only people to question what our bodies will be like after death. The people of Bible days had the same question, asking: "How are the dead raised? And with what kind of body do they come?" (1 Cor. 15:35). So Paul answered, writing about the spiritual body in 1 Corinthians 15:35–54. (If you have time, open your Bible and read through this passage right now.)

Today the questions take on varying forms of the original. "What will this body look like? How will it function? Will it be better than the temporary tissue we surrendered in order to enter heaven's timelessness?" We can be quite sure our new body will be zit-free, fat-free, and gravity free. But what is it, exactly? The Bible reveals several characteristics of our heavenly body. Let's take a look.

It's truly original

You do not sow the body which is to be ... but God gives it a body just as He wished.

—1 Corinthians 15:37–38

The Bible talks about two bodies, an earthly and a heavenly body. (I already have two bodies, and I'm trying to get back down to one. I'm trying to get down to 168 pounds, which was my birth weight. But I digress.) Scripture uses the understanding we have of our natural body to validate the existence of the spiritual

> **I already have two bodies, and I'm trying to get back down to one.**

body. This comparison helps us in our basic understanding of the spirit body, even though the spirit body isn't patterned after our physical body. We have two hands attached to two arms, as well as two feet connected at the ends of two legs. We have internal organs and miles of nerves and blood vessels. Our spiritual body may have a similar outward appearance (or it may not), but the internal organs will most certainly be different, if they are even present at all.

The shape our earthly body is in does not serve as the template for our spiritual, heavenly body (and everyone lets out a great sigh of relief). If a guy dies by exploding at a pie-eating contest, his spiritual body doesn't have star-shaped scars on the stomach, and it isn't a hundred pounds overweight. If somebody else dies with forty-seven marshmallows in her mouth, the cheeks of her spiritual body will not be pouched out. Or if another person dies of suppository overdose ... well you get the idea. Our earthly body is distinct and separate from our heavenly spiritual body. It serves only as a recognizable reference point to help us begin to

> " If a guy dies by exploding at a pie-eating contest, his spiritual body doesn't have star-shaped scars on the stomach, and it isn't a hundred pounds overweight. "

understand and accept the reality of this spirit body.

Our new body is not a fixer-upper. It is pre-designed and specifically cre-ated for eternity. The body God gives us is not a

> 66 Some actually fear that we'll all be re-created as clones of Christ. The only thing I have to say about this is: That's too creepy and *Children of the Corn*-ish. 99

do-it-yourself kit with some assembly required. It comes com-pletely assembled, fully charged, and ready for use.

It's identifiable Some people worry that our heavenly bodies will be nondescript or indefinable. They wonder whether they'll be able to recognize anyone, or whether others will be able to recognize them. Our eternal body will be identifiable by others in heaven. It will surely look different, but it will not be offensive. We will see and be seen, know and be known.

It's individual When people talk with me about this subject, they also express concern over everyone looking the same. Some actually fear that we'll all be re-created as clones of Christ. The only thing I have to say about this is: That's too creepy and *Children of the Corn*-ish, and that if our loving Creator had enough originality to produce millions of different kinds of plants and animals, and to make even the molecules and the atoms distinct (not to mention fingerprints and snowflakes), then how can anyone really think that he would resort to cloning? Surely God will individualize our new, timeless bodies.

It's indestructible Our eternal body will never get sick, never break out or down. We'll suffer no more broken bones, cancer, or any other disease. And we will finally be done with that annoying red skin that comes with daily shaving.

> **"We'll be able to eat whatever we want, just as long as it's in the food-chain of heaven. "**

And get this: no more conflict between the flesh and the spirit! No longer will our body want to do one thing and our spirit the other (see Rom. 7:14–24). Completing the will of God will be our natural desire rather than just feeding or caring for a body. Our preoccupation with staying in shape will end. We'll be able to eat whatever we want, just as long as it's in the food-chain of heaven.

It's immeasurable God creates our spiritual body for heavenly existence. This timeless body is a life container created by God to forever hold the life he has given us. Our earthly bodies were never capable of unending survival; they were meant to wear out and die while performing tasks in our earthly environment. But we need a new body in order to survive in the environment of heaven. We will receive our new body on the other side of death, and it will never wear out and never die.

> *For we know that if the earthly tent which is our house is torn down, we have a building from God, a house not made with hands, eternal in the heavens. For indeed in this house we groan, longing to be clothed with our dwelling from heaven.*
>
> —2 Corinthians 5:1–2

God designed our natural body to contain and fulfill the life Jesus gives us while on earth. Without Jesus, our earthly life containers are underutilized and under-filled. These natural bodies were created with all the qualities necessary to carry out and fulfill the complete work God has planned for mankind to do.

Because our responsibilities and duties change once we get to heaven, our bodies will be different, too. They will have all the qualities necessary to carry out our new duties as assigned in heaven. There will be some similarities, but the differences will be welcomed.

The verse above mentions that our earthly bodies long to be clothed in our new heavenly body. The limitations of our earthly bodies will vanish when we receive these new spiritual bodies. What will it be

> 66 What will it be like finally to be free of cellulite? 99

like to be free from the limitations our bodies now impose on us? What will it be like finally to be free of cellulite? Our natural body harbors so much weakness until the inevitable, death. But our spiritual body exudes health, power, and life eternal.

It's thoroughly outfitted

raised in glory

—1 Corinthians 15:43

Our new bodies come fully equipped with the total package mirroring God's attributes. These attributes are not options to be selected like the touring package on a new vehicle. Let's look at this standard equipment more closely. Here's what's included:

God's construction God is spirit, and we will be remade into spirit beings. This doesn't mean our bodies will be ghostly. It means that the fundamental construct of our existence will be changed from the physical to the spiritual. In Genesis, the Bible says God created mankind in his own image. This means he created us as reflector versions of himself. In the life after life, we will be re-created to be like God is.

God's content God makes his choices based on his all-knowingness. His knowledge and wisdom encompass the full scope of eternity, and he will place within each of us his own content of knowledge. We won't know everything God knows, of course. But we will have an eternal scope of history from which to base the decisions for our activities.

God's character True strength comes from authentic character. While we are on the earth, we strive to discipline and control ourselves in order to develop as much of the character of God as possible. When we receive our timeless bodies, they'll come complete with the whole of God's character—

• *Truthfulness.* We will think and speak as God does. Everything he speaks is truth, and everything he thinks is truth.

• *Goodness.* These are the things God approves. The only things that will come out of us are the things God approves.

• *Love.* This unselfish, non-judgmental motivation originates from God and is the atmosphere permeating everything in heaven.

• *Peace.* God is completely content with who he is. He doesn't have a mid-life crisis. He doesn't need to make himself feel better by creating another earth where everyone drives red sports cars and dates young blondes. The peace we search for in the people we know, the possessions we own, and the power we've gathered becomes full and complete in the peace of God. No longer will we sense the need for peace, it will be a permanent inseparable part of our makeup.

> 66 We will have more to do than just sit around in the clouds playing harps. There is an eternity of work to do. 99

These attributes become ours the instant we enter heaven. They are not something we grow into after receiving our timeless body and learning how to use it. They are not skills that we develop after living in our new body for a few millennia. The Bible says we are transformed in "a moment." The original biblical Greek word for a *moment* gives us our English word "atom." In other words, we receive our new, fully functioning body in an instant so minuscule that it can't be perceived.

Our lives on earth are splintered into microscopic pieces, all demanding the best we have to offer. Work, family, friends, and church are only a few of the larger pieces that make up most of the more important demands. Most of us feel so scattered that we wonder if we are really making a difference in any of these areas. Or are the small, multiple investments we make more of a detriment than a help?

The body God has prepared for us will be totally occupied with only one thing: the accomplishment of God's will. We receive this body not for our own pleasure or self-enhancement but finally to become everything we were created for. We will be in heaven, and we will have more to do than just sit around in

> 66 Understanding these things requires that our finite brains stretch beyond what they are capable of grasping: the infinite. 99

the clouds playing harps. There is an eternity of work to do, and we will each have our assignment.

It's task oriented

raised in power

—1 Corinthians 15:43

Revelation 21 speaks about heaven by calling it a city, the new Jerusalem. Heaven is a city, and we will be its citizens. We are not called to live out eternal life in isolation and loneliness, sitting around bored and idle. There is always something new and exciting to see and experience. The city is always changing.

In the heavenly city, all kinds of people work together, depend on each other, and cooperate in order to share in common responsibility. The city has room for individuality, and life will unfold the way God designed it to be lived. Heaven is not an eternal retirement resort, not "Leisure Landing," where everyone drives golf carts to the store and to church. It's a place where there will always be new things to learn, new things to do, and new tasks to perform in service to the living God.

When our earthly life is over, and we step into eternity, we have a great deal more to look forward to than just millions of years looking at the same people, singing the same songs, and never needing sleep. There is a real life with adventure and excitement awaiting us. God is up to something far greater than anything we have seen or experienced this side of heaven. The greatest, most exciting experiences we have ever had or dreamed about will seem tame when compared to the tasks waiting for us in heaven.

I know that as you read this sitting in a tangible reality, it is difficult to even begin to conceptualize these things. They seem far out, and it's hard to imagine living for all eternity. So let me share a story that might help. I live in Oklahoma City. It is not a bad place to live, but there's not a lot to see, because it's very flat. There's one place where you can stand and actually see the curvature of the earth!

> **Eternity is more than the passage of time. ... Rather than a quantity ... it's a quality of life.**

Oklahoma has lots of small towns that are very dull, and their names reflect what goes on there. One of these is a place called Poteau (pronounced "Poe-toe"). First of all, doesn't that name say it all? If you knew you had one more day to live, you might go to Poteau—after all, one day in Poteau feels like an eternity.

But here's my point: Eternity is more than the passage of time. In fact, eternity will outlast the batteries in the world's atomic clock. Eternity has no beginning and it has no end; we just get the privilege of jumping in and never jumping out. Rather than a *quantity*, then, it's a *quality* of life.

The purpose of having a body in heaven is to live eternal life. Even eternal life has a purpose that is the eternal fulfillment of God's will. Once we step across the invisible border through death, we begin eternity with a new life, a new body, a new mind, and a new purpose. Understanding these things requires that our finite brains stretch beyond what they are capable of grasping: the infinite. But when we do step into heaven's eternity, we will do so knowing each other, comfortable in our new bodies, understanding our new tasks, and seeing Christ face to face, just as he is.

Chapter Five

CAN WE TALK TO THE DEAD?

C able TV, hundreds of channels, and nothing entertaining to watch. Have you noticed? By the time I get back to my hotel room after speaking, it's late, and there's always a show on where the host is talking with dead people. These hosts claim to be psychics and mediums.

The other night I watched one of these guys address his audience while hunting for a couple of willing participants. After the intro music faded, the applause died down, the lights dimmed, and he closed his eyes as if trying to hear something that was making no noise—or see something that normal people could not see. "I'm hearing a great many voices, all talking at the same time ... trying to focus in on just one ... *Sit* ... I hear the word *Sit*, or is it *Sat?* The many voices are now gone ... only silence ... wait, I'm getting ... *Wam* ... *Wam* ... not the sound, but the word, *Wam.* ... Does that mean anything to someone in our audience tonight?"

A middle-aged man raised his hand, and the host

encouraged him to speak. The overhead boom microphone swung to capture the man's words. "Those are my uncle's initials!" The audience was amazed, and a soft murmur rolled across the room. "Walter Allen Matthews, that's my uncle's initials. He died in World War Two." Again, the murmur, but a bit louder this time.

The host nods and closes his eyes once again. "Listening ... waiting ... nothing but sile—" He breaks his word in half to repeat what he has heard. "I'm hearing the word, *Dymund ... Dymon ... Diamond*,—that's it, *Diamond*. A woman speaks from the front row, "Before he died, my husband was the president of Neil Diamond's national fan club for over ten years." Once again the audience members voice their approval of the obvious giftedness of their host.

Encouraged by the audience's outpouring of appreciation, he continues; "I'm hearing something else ... quiet please ... I'm hearing, *Keal Am Peye ... Keal Am Peye*. Does anyone recognize anything about these words? I'm speaking the words exactly as I'm hearing them spoken from the other side: *Keal Am Peye* ... anyone? Do these words make a connection with anyone in our audience?" The audience remains silent, stunned that the host had missed. "No one?" he says, one last time.

The audience exhibits a bit of anxiety for its host, wondering if he can recover from such an obvious miss. The host smiles, "Mine is not an exact science; it is a gift much like that of the master musician who occasionally misplays a note." The audience chuckles, and he successfully wins back their confidence. He closes his eyes; the audience members take silent breaths.

"Mmmmm ... ahhhh ... yessssss ... *Heaven* ... I hear something about *Heaven*." The audience sighs and seems to smile in unison. Just hearing the word brings comfort to everyone gathered in the studio. "We all know someone there, don't we?" The host lifts his hands overhead and allows his gaze to follow. The audience applauds and cheers his gifted revelation.

"Now I'm hearing their words more quickly and with much less effort. I'm hearing something that sounds like ... *Drill* ... does anyone relate with the word *Drill?* One of the younger audience members, who hadn't been tuned in quite as keenly as the rest, suddenly joins the group when she hears that word.

> "I was too busy making my own comment, 'I'll take Liquids that Are Absent from Hell for $1,000, Alex.'"

She turns to the person sitting next to her and says in a not-so-quiet voice, "I hate going to the dentist, don't you?"

The pace of the host's meditation quickens. *"Churches,"* he calls out. Immediately an audience member responds, "My great-grandfather was a circuit preacher!" The host continues, *"Frank."* Another audience member calls out, "My first dog was named Frank!" The host begins to perspire, *"Water."*

I didn't hear what the audience member said at that point. I was too busy making my own comment, "I'll take Liquids that Are Absent from Hell for $1,000, Alex." I was tired and ready for sleep, so I reached for the remote just as the host said, "One more ... I'm hearing ... *Mentos.*"

I sat there thinking about what I had just seen. The host of a nationally syndicated TV show listening to dead people talk and trying to make some sense of it with his studio audience. It's true that something is happening on "the other side." But no living human is in the position to see clearly what it is. The best we can do is guess.

Guessing is what this TV host was doing. I have no doubt he heard dead people talking, but he didn't understand what was *really* happening. The speakers' comments made no immediate sense to him, because all he could hear were snippets of conversations without a context.

> **The real action was occurring in a large carpeted room with enough chairs for the twenty or thirty dead people milling around talking with each other.**

The real action was occurring in a large carpeted room with enough chairs for the twenty or thirty dead people milling around talking with each other. The leader for the evening went to the front of the room and, in a loud voice, said, "Sit down everyone. Come on, it's time to play. Everybody take a seat." Two dead guys were still by the refreshment table, swapping stories when the leader called over: "John, *sit!*"

When everyone had finally taken their seats, the leader explained that the group game for the evening was Mad-Libs. He explained the rules. "I'll call out a type of word that I need, and everyone calls out that type of word. I'll write it in the blank on the Mad-Lib book, and when all the blanks are filled in, I'll read the funny story."

Everyone understood, so the leader began the game. "I need a word that makes a funny sound."

"Wham" came the quick response.

The leader wrote the word in the first blank. "Next, I need a baseball term."

"Diamond," someone said from the middle of the room.

"That's a good one," the leader chuckled. "Now I need a type of dessert." Several suggestions were offered, but the leader took the one he liked best: *Key Lime Pie.*

"Now give me a place where you'd most like to be," the leader instructed.

Someone on his right said, *"Heaven,"* and the rest of the room nodded in sad agreement. In order not to lose the group in the emotion of the moment, the leader quickly said, "Now give me the name of a tool."

"Richard Simmons" was the quickest response, and it brought a big laugh out of everyone. But the leader wrote down: *Drill.*

"Okay, only four more to go. Give me the name of a fast-food restaurant."

"Church's Fried Chicken" was the answer everyone liked the best.

"Now give me something that goes well with beans."

The group thought for just a moment before coming up with *"Franks."*

"Now I need the name of a liquid."

"Water" was the first answer; it was also the best.

"Now for the last one. Give me the name of a candy."

Two or three of the dead said at the same time, *"Mentos."*

•••

The Gallup Poll says 37 percent of us believe it's possible to talk to the dead. Psychics have reported that their income has grown to over $500 million a year from just speaking to the dead. In addition to the TV shows, and the mediums in almost every town, countless telephone psychic services will supposedly assist the inquirer with a direct line to the dead. Their phone number should be 900-543-8663 (900-LIE-TOME), because that's all anyone calling these services should expect.

> **When people talk to the dead, they are opening themselves up to something truly dangerous.**

There's apparently so much talking between the world of the living and the world of the dead! But can we really dial up anybody we want, at any time? Looking at it from a biblical viewpoint will help us with this often muddled topic. There is, indeed, a supernatural world filled with all sorts of spiritual beings. Forces intent on destroying us exist in this realm. When people talk to the dead, they are opening themselves up to something truly dangerous. Take these words to heart:

> *There shall not be found among you anyone who ...*
> *uses divination, one who practices witchcraft, or one*
> *who interprets omens, or a sorcerer, or one who casts a*
> *spell, or a medium, or a spiritist, or one who calls up*
> *the dead.*

—Deuteronomy 18:10–11

People have always been desperate to hang onto things they have lost, especially loved ones. Whether it is a parent or a grandparent, a child or a sibling, they have lost someone they consider essential if their own life is to continue. These unresolved feelings of *abandonment* are probably the most basic motivation for wanting to talk with the dead.

Loneliness is the second most common reason for people wanting to communicate with "the other side." In life, personalities become intertwined and interdependent. Loneliness can drive a person to do almost anything to carry on the relationship. Spouses, for example, want to

66 Talking with 'the other side' is possible, but it is banned in Scripture. 99

find out how their partner is doing over there. In reality, though, they are simply lonely.

Curiosity is a third powerful motivator that misleads many into talking with the dead. After all, a natural curiosity has always surrounded death. We do want to know what to expect at our own death.

Whether it's a sense of abandonment, loneliness, or curiosity—regardless of the motivation—talking with "the other side" is possible, but it is banned in Scripture. Why? Because there are great dangers in it. See for yourself—

It grants entrance to deception

Saul said to his servants, "Seek for me a woman who is a medium, that I may go to her and inquire of her."

—1 Samuel 28:7

There was a time in his life when Saul experienced the full favor of God. If you remember your Old Testament history, you'll recall that priest Samuel sought the counsel of God and chose Saul to be the first king of Israel. During the years of favor, Saul also sought the counsel of God for just about any situation he faced. But over time, Saul allowed himself to indulge in certain things he had publicly declared illegal.

Even though he had outlawed mediums and psychics from the land, the Bible reveals his desire to talk with the dead. On the surface of his kingship, he created the appearance of compliance with the Word of God. But in his personal life, he dabbled in many of the things he had prohibited.

After several years, Samuel died, and Saul thus lost his godly advisor. Now the armies of Israel faced what could be the most significant battle of Saul's career as king. He needed to know what to do, but Samuel was not there to ask. What did Saul do? He sought out a medium who could allow him to speak to the dead Samuel. Saul's irrationality now became evident, as did the depth of his deception.

Saul hid himself in layers of clothes. Making himself look like a commoner, he entered the medium's tent and asked her to conjure up anyone he chose in order to speak with them. Saul wasn't uncomfortable making this request, but the medium seemed a bit uneasy, especially when she realized who was making the request.

> **" Saul's experience tells me this: Talking with the dead grants entrance to deception. "**

The medium began to call up Samuel and was frightened at what she saw. She said, "I see a divine spirit-being rising up out of the earth, an old man dressed in grave clothes." Saul couldn't see what the medium saw, so he placed absolute trust in a complete stranger, virtually placing the welfare of his armies—and the entire nation—in her hands!

Saul desperately wanted to believe that Samuel would

come to him from death. So, as soon as the medium began to describe what she saw (and called it Samuel herself), he identified the spirit as Samuel. However, I believe the spirit rising out of the ground was not Samuel, but a demon dressed in grave clothes. I say this because I'm convinced (along with such theological greats as Luther and Calvin) that it is "impossible that God should allow his prophet to be the victim of diabolical sorceries."[1] Because of the intense superstition of his life, Saul had opened the door to full-scale deception. Instead of seeking advice from God, he was now seeking advice from a spirit conjured up by a witch.

> **The dark forces roaming the world are not interested in helping us discover anything other than new ways to make our lives more ineffective.**

Saul's experience tells me this: Talking with the dead grants entrance to deception. Yet talking with the dead is a multimillion-dollar industry today, and growing every year. What concerns me the most is the number of believers being fooled. They demonstrate their own deception by agreeing with three of the most popular beliefs regarding the afterlife.

That disembodied spirits roam the earth This belief promotes the thinking that after people die, their disembodied spirits simply roam the earth and can be contacted. The only problem with this belief is that it's not scriptural. Disembodied spirits don't roam the world; dark forces do. People who embrace this belief are dangerously close to hugging demons.

That we should communicate with the dead This is the idea that we *need* to communicate with these spirits. Just because we *can* communicate with them doesn't mean that we should. The dark forces roaming the world are not interested in helping us discover anything other than new ways to make our lives more ineffective. Any communication with the dead is really communication with dark forces. The result is deception.

That the dead can direct us This belief promotes the idea that because the dead exist in a dimension different from ours, they have the ability to see things we cannot. The truth is that contacting these spirits in order to gain greater insight into anything is like reading a book through the glass in a welder's mask. You end up knowing less than before you started!

Anyone who tries to talk with the dead opens himself up to serious deception. At the same time, talking with the dead flies in the face of what really happens at the moment of death.

It goes against the evidence of death

And he said, "Bring up Samuel for me."

—1 Samuel 28:11

When Saul asked the medium to conjure up Samuel for him, she described a dark force rising up out of the ground, dressed in grave clothes. Saul immediately identified this force as being Samuel, just as people assume their psychic is talking about their spouse—just because the psychic mentions something about snoring, and Bubba occasionally snored like two mating elk. (I've never personally witnessed the mating rituals of elk ... but you get the idea.)

Saul was not speaking with Samuel; he was speaking with a dark force that had come to fulfill the irrational belief Saul had developed that he could, in fact, talk with the dead. The woman was no doubt more than willing to go along with it all.

> Dark forces don't just show up in our lives with long handled sickles. They could be wearing a Raiders jacket and a pair of UGGS.

You see, it's actually impossible to speak with the dead, because of the three basic events that take place at the instant of death.

There is imminent destruction "For we know that if the earthly tent which is our house is torn down, we have a building from God, a house not made with hands, eternal in the heavens" (2 Cor. 5:1). Once death occurs, the body begins a rapid process of decay. If not protected by a mortician, there will be imminent destruction of the tissue.

There is instant departure "We are of good courage, I say, and prefer rather to be absent from the body and to be at home with the Lord" (2 Cor. 5:8). The instant death happens, our spirit departs the body. Our body has roamed the earth, but our spirit doesn't; it instantly departs the body and leaves the earth.

There is an immediate destination "The poor man died and was carried away by the angels to Abraham's bosom; and the rich man also died and was buried" (Luke 16:22). The moment after death our spirit departs the earth for its new home, either with God or separated from him. Immediately after death we are either with the Lord or without Him.

Whomever Saul was talking with that day in the medium's tent, it was most likely not Samuel. Samuel had encountered the three unavoidable experiences of death. The main reason we shouldn't talk with the dead is because when we do, we're not talking with the dead!

We might be talking with dark forces intent on even greater deception in our lives. Dark forces don't just show up in our lives with long handled sickles. They could be wearing a Raiders jacket and a pair of LUGS. They might tell you to devote your life to following Tony Robbins, or they might show up asking, "What's a nice girl like you doing in a place like this?"

It is grounds for extreme damage

"Tomorrow you and your sons will be with me.
Indeed the LORD will give over the army of Israel into
the hands of the Philistines!"

—1 Samuel 28:19

This is a powerful Old Testament story dealing directly with the subject of talking with the dead. The key to understanding it comes in verse 6. "When Saul inquired of the Lord, the Lord did not answer him, either by dreams or by Urim or by prophets." Saul had so betrayed his calling as God's chosen king for Israel that God had removed his presence from him. Now when Saul inquired of the Lord, the only answer he received was ... silence.

> **The question that explodes in my mind is: 'Up from where?'**

When Saul first became king, he was careful to inquire of God before he made decisions, and he was careful to do the things God told him to do. He had banned all mediums in the land, but later in his career, when he found himself abandoned by God, he hungered for wisdom from beyond this life. He found that his own knowledge often came up short. He craved the advice of Samuel and said to the necromancer: "Bring him up for me!"

The first words Saul heard were: "Why have you disturbed me by bringing me up?"

The question that explodes in my mind is: "Up from *where?*" Let's handle this question with geography. We basically think of heaven as being above and hell being below, right? So if something or someone came *up,* where would this person or this thing be

> " God does *not* encourage, permit, or endorse the use of spiritists, mediums, or psychics. "

coming from? It would not be coming up from heaven but from much further south of there.

This whole encounter is not coming from God. He did not originate it or condone it. I believe the witch contacted an evil spirit that was wrapped up in a robe. It is not Samuel; Saul assumed that it was Samuel because of his belief in the witch's abilities to conjure up the dead. Neither the witch nor Saul could honestly determine who had joined their party. Notice what the evil spirit says—it was speaking in generalities about Saul. Anyone could have known the information he was giving.

The entire point of this story is that God does *not* encourage, permit, or endorse the use of spiritists, mediums, or psychics. He knows that doing so opens up a clear path for that person to converse with an evil spirit, whose sole purpose is to destroy life and take eternal prisoners.

Saul chose to ignore the scriptural prohibitions regarding

consulting mediums. He chose instead to seek advice he felt he needed at any cost. Little did he know that it would cost him his life. This would be his epitaph:

> *So Saul died for his trespass which he committed against the LORD, because of the word of the LORD which he did not keep; and also because he asked counsel of a medium, making inquiry of it, and did not inquire of the LORD. Therefore He [God] killed him and turned the kingdom to David the son of Jesse.*
>
> —1 Chronicles 10:13–14

66 **But why talk with the dead when we can have unlimited face time with the living Creator, God himself?** 99

Besides being weird, seeking to contact the dead violates some very real biblical guidelines. (For example, check out these verses: Deut. 18:10–12; Lev. 19:31; Isa. 8:19.) First, it ignores biblical warnings against the use of mediums and psychics. It's impossible for God to be any clearer: "Don't have anything to do with it!" Second, it assumes that God would prefer to speak to us through the dead rather than through his Word or prayer. Third, it implies that God sends dead people on his behalf to speak with us.

The biblical prohibitions are set up for our protection. If we are contemplating talking with the dead, we ought to think again! The only thing that will show up will be a demonic spirit, and the only thing it will give is a dark forecast. When we violate biblical guidelines, we stir up demonic forces that we have no idea how to handle. When God needs to speak to us, he will use his Word, the Bible, and his Holy Spirit.

Can we talk with the dead? Yes. When we do, we are talking to the eternally dead, those demonic spirits who have been assigned by Satan to carry out his orders and fulfill his will. But why talk with the dead when we can have unlimited face time with the living Creator, God himself? If we're talking with the dead, we're not talking with God.

Chapter Six

WHY DIE TWICE?

Congratulations! If you've made it this far into the book, you're not dead yet. Even so, there are some signs you *might* be dead ...

- If you're lying on a table with bright lights in your face, and you hear one medical student say to another, "Hey, I didn't get to shock him yet. It's *my* turn!"
- You're flashing your KKK tattoo at a 50 Cent concert.
- You've been married for twenty-four years, only to discover that what you thought was love could be cured by Prozac.
- You're traveling rapidly toward a bright light at the end of a tunnel when you realize you're driving the wrong way in a one-way underpass ... and a word printed over the light suddenly comes into focus: "Amtrak."

- As the crowd cheers you on, you volunteer for a knife-throwing trick at a traveling circus. Walking past the knife thrower, you smell alcohol on his breath.
- You can't see your relatives as they walk by, because you thought helmets were for sissies.
- Your new home is a metal urn placed on the mantel, right next to the Precious Moments figurines.
- As you groggily watch your grandfather slip peacefully into the afterlife, you are quickly stirred by the reality that you've been dozing in the backseat ... and Gramps is driving.

As long as we still draw breath—and we really aren't dead yet—we can choose what to do with our lives. Here's the interesting thing about it: *The choices we make this side of death determine whether or not we die twice.* You see, everyone will die once, whether from old age, an accident, or someone else's stupidity. We will all, one day, stop breathing. At that moment we will either face eternal life or the second death. Separation from God is the second death.

> **At that moment we will either face eternal life or the second death.**

To better understand this subject, we need to listen closely to the words of Jesus about it. His words in Scripture reveal to us several truths regarding the second death.

Heaven isn't fair

"Your kingdom come. Your will be done, on earth as it is in heaven."

—Matthew 6:10

Fair is for balls hit with bats, states in the early fall, or love and war. But it's not for heaven. Heaven isn't designed to be fair, because God always gets his way there. No committees, no votes. Therefore, God doesn't even need veto power.

When we get to heaven, we won't line up with the other new arrivals for that day, wait for the starter's signal, and then run to find our god. There is only one God in heaven, the One who created it to perfectly carry out his will.

So, heaven isn't egalitarian. It is, however, theocratic. There are no protests in heaven. Angels don't sign petitions against the incessant domination of God's will above their own. There are no picket lines, sit-ins, or million angel marches. None of these things will happen, because heaven is *not* egalitarian. It

> **There are no protests in heaven. Angels don't sign petitions against the incessant domination of God's will above their own. There are no picket lines, sit-ins, or million angel marches.**

is the exclusive domain of God. In fact, Scripture mentions three types of heaven:

Creation parade Genesis 1 tells us that before there was time, God created the planets (including the earth), the moon, and the stars. He referred to these created bodies as the heavens. We still refer to "the heavens" when we talk about looking into space.

Cosmic province Old Testament Jacob left home to start his own life. One night, while Jacob was asleep in a field (see Genesis 23), he saw a ladder reaching from the earth into heaven, and angels were ascending and descending on the ladder. In his vision, he saw angels coming in and out of the world.

But this supernatural world is normally intangible to us humans; we can't see it or touch it. This is the place where the angels dwell, and it is also called heaven. It is a place where God's angels and Satan's forces fight it out regarding God's will. Here incredible supernatural battles rage, and the prize is the control of all earthly creation, including man.

66 **This won't be a cosmic 'Trading Spaces,' where the angels and mankind redo each other's dimensions.** 99

Crown place The third heaven is the highest heaven, the place where God sits on his throne. This is the epicenter of heaven where

110

all eternal activity originates. Here all of humankind will ultimately stand before God. The apostle Paul ascended to this place but wasn't permitted to speak about the things he heard and saw there (see 2 Cor. 12:2–4).

In the crown place God accomplishes all of his purposes, no matter how the human being lives in the creation parade (and this free-thinking, free-choosing creature quite often chooses to do his own will rather than God's). In the cosmic province, God's angels constantly compete with dark forces for the accomplishment of God's will. But there will be an instant when God stops time. At that moment, he'll create a new heaven and a new earth.

> " Fair is for balls hit with bats, states in the early fall, or love and war. But it's not for heaven. "

This won't be a cosmic "Trading Spaces," where the angels and mankind redo each other's dimensions. It is the creation of an entirely new earth and an entirely new heaven. For the first time, God will have his complete way in all three places! The three levels of heaven will come together and be fashioned into a new city—the eternal, holy city of God. In this new place, the will of God will hold full sway.

Both the earth we know, and the supernatural world existing just beyond our comprehension, are in such turmoil because egalitarianism and fairness dominate these places. Satan's competing agenda struggles to stifle God's will. And on the earth, humankind seeks self-awareness and self-expression. When these two levels of heaven are re-created and conjoined with the crown room, the turmoil will cease. Why? Because all our superficial notions of egalitarianism and fairness will end. For it will be the new city where God's will constantly reigns supreme.

The apostle John wrote the Book of Revelation and described heaven mostly in negatives. Rather than trying to convey the infinite splendor of heaven with a limited human vocabulary, John chose to link the celestial realities with the realities of human existence. He identified ten negative qualities of life and asked the reader to imagine a place where these did *not* exist. The absence of these negatives make the eternal positives possible.

No loneliness Heaven will be anything but lonely. There will be three groups of people in heaven. First, those who remain loyal to Christ amidst the trials of earthly life (see Luke 22:28–30). Second, the martyrs for Christ, those who lost their lives for refusing to reject him. Third, the overcomers among the churches. These are the people who do the will of God all the way up

> " In heaven, we get an eternal pass on death. Just imagine: fearless bungee jumping and extreme hacky-sack! "

to the end of their lives. *A new community will welcome us the moment we arrive.*

No hunger or thirst Our new bodies will no longer require the regular feeding like our mortal bodies did. Food and drink may be a part of heaven, but they are not key ingredients to the sustenance of eternal life. Our relationship with Christ sustains our heavenly life. *A new passion is exchanged for food* (see Rev. 7:16).

No sea Throughout the Scripture, water often symbolizes the presence and activity of evil in the world. When the Scripture says there is no more sea, it is saying there is no longer any evil. *A new rightness displaces all evil* (see Rev. 21:1).

No tears There will be no physical pain, no emotional pain, and no tears. Nothing will ever make us cry again. Gone are the bad days and the negative feelings. Gone are depression and anxiety. *A new contentment is traded for our sorrows* (see Rev. 21:4).

No death Dreaded and feared—prepared for, yet totally unexpected—death is the one sure experience all humans share. When anyone dies, they leave others behind along with a laundry list of uncompleted tasks, dreams, and activities. Death is the most popular thing to procrastinate! In heaven, we get an eternal pass on death. Just imagine: fearless bungee jumping and extreme hacky-sack! *A new animation no longer conceptualizes death* (see Rev. 21:4).

No pain Heaven is the only place where the physical pains we bear in our bodies will be gone. There will be no need for medicine, surgery, or artificial limbs. We will all have new bodies that never feel pain. *A new wholeness makes pain extinct* (see Rev. 21:4).

No temple No longer will there be any need for special buildings to house gathered worshipers. God himself will be the temple, as he himself will be the eternal house for heaven's citizens. No more building funds and "Forever We Build" programs! *God Himself is our refuge of worship* (see Rev. 21:22).

No sun or moon All the light we have on the earth originates from some limited source. Our sun only has so much stored energy. A light bulb will only burn for so many hours. But in heaven the light of God permeates every corner, forever. *A permanent unquenchable light illuminates all of eternity* (see Rev. 21:23).

> " One of the most profound truths is that hell is an actual place. "

No alarms The gates of heaven will never close because there is no need. The gates of ancient cities closed when evil approached. Because evil can't exist in heaven, the gates of heaven will never close. *An impenetrable shield of security surrounds us* (see Rev. 21:25).

114

No night God created the night to allow us to sleep and renew ourselves for another day. In heaven, there will be no need for rest because we will never grow weary or tired. *A new energy is transfused into our veins* (see Rev. 22:5).

John's list of heaven's missing features is the ultimate wish list for everyone. When God gets his way, the absence of these things makes for the perfect environment. Heaven isn't fair by all our standards, but it sure is a great place to live.

Hell is final

"[He] shall be guilty enough to go into the fiery hell."

—Matthew 5:22

The Bible describes hell in various ways, but one of the most profound truths is that hell is an actual place. To Jesus, hell was a location, an environment God never intended humans ever to experience. It's not just a nightmare implanted into the minds of gullible people to instill fear. It's not just a fairytale story aimed at controlling behavior. Hell is the place where all rebellion and disobedience will be housed for all eternity. It is completely removed from God and his orderly creation. It is the final resting-place of everything de-created. Let's look closer at the essence of hell.

Hell is the antithesis of creation "If your right eye makes you stumble, tear it out and throw it from you; for it is better for you to lose one of the parts of your body, than for your whole body to be thrown into hell. If your right hand makes you stumble, cut it off and throw it from you; for it is better for you to lose one of the parts of your body, than for your whole body to go into hell" (Matt. 5:29–30).

God created life. Satan and his competing agenda sought every way to *de*-create life. God created man in complete freedom; through his lies and deceit, Satan robbed man of his freedom. God created a world, and when he looked upon it he said that it was perfect. Satan immediately set about the task

> 66 God is the Creator; Satan is the destroyer. Heaven is life, but hell is death, the antithesis of creation. 99

of de-creating this perfect creation. God is the Creator; Satan is the destroyer. Heaven is life, but hell is death, the antithesis of creation.

You'll find many metaphors in the Bible to describe hell. These comparisons give us deeper insight into its realities. I have found it interesting that the Scripture actually uses *contrasting* metaphors to great effect:

- **Total darkness**—and fire.
- **The pit**—and a burning lake.
- **A place of punishment**—and destruction.
- **Cast *out***—and cast *down*.
- **Gnashing of teeth**—and sorrow.

These metaphors show us a place that is the exact opposite of what God desires for his people. When Jesus referred to hell, he referred to a long, narrow valley just outside Jerusalem's walls where the city's garbage was dumped and burned. The fire of the dump never went out, and every day, people piled more refuse on top to be burned. Nothing thrown into the valley was ever redeemed; it was doomed for the fire. Jesus likened this valley to hell, only he was careful to point out that hell was ... *much worse.*

Hell is the dumping ground of the cosmos, the cosmic refuse dump. Everything de-created is forever doomed for hell. God creates life, Satan de-creates it, and hell is the recipient of wasted life.

Hell is against God's character "The Lord is ... patient toward you, not wishing for any to perish but for all to come to repentance" (2 Peter 3:9). The character of God is not geared toward retribution or punishment but compassion and forgiveness. He is willing to do anything necessary to minimize the number of people who waste life and end up in the cosmic refuse. God's character drives him to minimize loss and maximize the number of those who find life. Without exception, God always acts in concert

> 66 We become the decisions we make, and it is our own personal decisions that place us in heaven or in hell. 99

with his character. It is completely misguided to think that God singles anyone out to go to hell. God wants no one to perish: "'For I have no pleasure in the death of anyone who dies,' declares the Lord GOD. 'Therefore, repent and live'" (Ezek. 18:32).

> ❝I'm amazed when people brag to me, 'I'm going to hell to party forever with my friends!'❞

Hell is actualized by our choices "Therefore God gave them over in the lusts of their hearts to impurity" (Rom. 1:24). He "gave them over." God doesn't send anyone to hell. Rather, we ourselves choose for or against life. Heaven exists to receive all who have chosen life. Hell receives all those who have chosen against life in favor of de-creation.

And be assured: God provides adequate opportunities for everyone to choose life. After enough of these opportunities are willfully ignored, God simply gives individuals up to the pursuit of their own de-creative ends. We become the decisions we make, and it is our own personal decisions that place us in heaven or in hell.

Hell is to be avoided at all costs "For I have five brothers—in order that he may warn them, so that they will not also come to this place of torment" (Luke 16:28). In Luke 16, we find the story of a rich man who died and went to hell. He lived his life in full pursuit of his own purposes and ends, and when he died, he found himself in complete separation from God, in the full grip of the second death.

I'm amazed when people brag to me, "I'm going to hell to party forever with my friends!" They laugh and poke each other, thinking that hell is one eternal rave. Instead, hell is more like the dumpster that never gets emptied. Hell is filled with the sight of mutilated corpses, human bones, maggots, flies, animals and birds stripping the flesh from dead bodies—as well as the smell of rotting and burning flesh. But hey, dude, *party on!*

Once the rich man fully realized he'd landed in the cosmic dumpster, he looked across an impassable chasm that forever separated him from God. And he pleaded with God to send someone to warn his brothers on earth about this horrible place. God replied that he had given everyone more than enough guidance to find the life he offered. They simply had to accept that life.

Here and now is the focus

Jesus' understanding of death permeated his life. He knew death was a reality for all of humankind, and he knew that he too would face it. But Jesus' philosophy was positive, not negative. It was filled with hope, focusing on the prize awaiting those who

> " The cost for following him has always been the same: lose your life in order to gain his life. "

died as holders of the life he came to bring. His understanding of death leads us to a new paradigm: No longer is death something to be postponed and avoided at all costs. Instead, we can see it as purposeful and beneficial as we develop our understanding of life. Specifically, here are four ways to understand death the way Jesus did:

Consider the cost of devotion "Whoever wishes to save his life will lose it" (Matt. 16:25). Jesus never quibbled over the price of following him. He told the twelve men he called disciples to leave everything they had and follow. He put the price of devotion right out front. He never used "loss leaders" to trick anyone into following him for a while before telling him the real cost. Anyone who wanted to bargain with Jesus over the cost soon found himself alone. And the cost for following him has always been the same: lose your life in order to gain his life.

> " Jesus' philosophy of death is that to gain life we must lose it. "

In its essence, losing life is turning one's back on death. Every one of us has developed an individual laundry list of what constitutes genuine life. Everything from "Places I want to go before I die," to "People I want to meet before *they* die." Accomplishments, purchases, experiences, and filled ledger sheets—all these and more comprise humankind's definition of real life. Then Jesus comes along and says, "If you want my life, you have to lose your life."

This is real repentance: letting go of everything you define as life and claiming only what Jesus defines as life. It can never be a "both/and" experience; it's always an "either/or." Losing life means that we switch strengths. We willfully switch our strength with his.

No only do we switch strengths, we also switch strategies. We stop pursuing the fulfillment of our defined life and seek the completion of his life in us. And not only is losing life turning one's back on death, it is also living as a Christ follower. The way we find life is by losing it; the way we live life is also by losing it. The twelve disciples left their boats, their businesses, and their busy lives to follow Jesus. They spent just a little over three years walking where he walked, sleeping where he slept, and eating what he ate. And when he was gone, the only thing they knew to do was to live life as he had shown them. If these twelve men were alive today, and we were to ask them what they gave up to follow Christ, their answer would be: "Nothing. I gave up nothing but gained everything I ever dreamed of."

Jesus' philosophy of death is that to gain life we must lose it. If we are to find the life that God created us to have, we must lose the life we have created for ourselves … and we must lose ourselves in the life he alone can give.

Calculate decisions "Do you suppose that these Galileans … [or] those eighteen on whom the tower in

Siloam fell and killed them were worse culprits than all the men who live in Jerusalem? I tell you, no, but unless you repent, you will all likewise perish" (Luke 13:2, 4–5). Jesus never assigned a moral reason for any death and never used death as a fear tactic. Instead, he pointed to death as a reason to focus on the here and now. He recalled this episode in Siloam and told the hearers that the deaths of these people should help them make better decisions while they themselves were still living.

> **Can you imagine standing in heaven, waiting your turn to meet Jesus, and the guy in front of you asks, 'How'd you get here?'**

Neither the Galileans who died (see Luke 13:2–5) nor the eighteen in Siloam were killed because they had lived extra-bad lives or because they had done some incredibly evil act. The Galileans had come to Jerusalem to worship, and they were murdered at the orders of Pilate. The eighteen were simply going about their day when the tower came crashing down on them. They weren't selling pornography or drugs or doing anything else wrong.

Can you imagine standing in heaven, waiting your turn to meet Jesus, and the guy in front of you asks, "How'd you get here?" You're still a bit surprised that you're standing in line to meet the King of Kings, but you answer his question just the same, "I was walking down the street minding my own business when I saw a Gentile coming my way—and before I could cross the sidewalk, the tower collapsed, killing me, the Gentile, and sixteen others."

Jesus was making the point that death serves as a watermark for life. The real question is not *why* did these people die in this way, but *how* did they live their lives before death? None of us knows when our death will come. It is vital that we make the most of our lives and live with the expectation that God will make his life full and complete in us. We must calculate the decisions we make in order to come most fully into agreement with God's continuously creative will.

> **Jesus teaches us that it is neither the internal nor the external, but the eternal that is worth the exchange of any person's soul.**

"For what will it profit a man if he gains the whole world and forfeits his soul? Or what will a man give in exchange for his soul?" (Matt. 16:26). The focus of our concentration ought to be the center of our soul. The exchange will be made one focal point at a time. Money, might, and a mark on generations to come is the pursuit of many. Bingo, bass fishing, and bowling are the blueprints others follow. Some people exchange everything for the external evidences that they are living the full life. Others trade all to achieve a harmonic internal balance within the circle of life. Jesus teaches us that it is neither the internal nor the external, but the eternal that is worth the exchange of any person's soul. Jesus would have us carefully calculate our decisions.

Celebrate the day "He is not the God of the dead, but of the living" (Mark 12:27). At almost every funeral, I hear the one-word question that has no perfect answer, "Why?" This question preoccupies everyone, regardless of whether the funeral is for an infant, or an old man, a businessman killed in an automobile accident, or a teenager on the practice fields after school. For many people, death invites the questioning of God's power and legitimacy.

> **We can celebrate our life because we don't have to live in fear of death. Death is not the end, but the beginning.**

Jesus did not use death in this way. He used death to point people to the truth that *God is the God of the living.* Once an individual dies, his eternity is sealed; he can make no more choices to affect eternity. All of these choices are made prior to death. The dead are eternally dead, but God is the God of the eternally alive. He is also the God of those on this earth whom he has made alive and is continually making alive.

We can celebrate our life because we don't have to live in fear of death. Death is not the end, but the beginning. And the here and now is our preparation for eternity. As believers, we need to live as if we know that God is the God of the living. We need to expect our lives to be the fullest and most meaningful of all humankind. After all, God is the creator and the primary celebrator of life, and he wants us to celebrate with him.

Consider destiny "Rather fear Him who is able to destroy both soul and body in hell" (Matt. 10:28). Jesus had respect for the death that he knew was approaching. He knew why he had come to earth, and while he respected his imminent death, he was not anxious for its arrival. Jesus taught us to respect death, but to have ultimate regard for God. We are told to fear (that is have ultimate regard for) the one who is able to cast your soul into hell, a.k.a. God.

In death, we all face what Jesus faced: loss of bodily control, loss of relationships, and (possibly) separation from the source of life (i.e., the second death).

Jesus' death experience gave him firsthand knowledge of these three aspects of death. When Jesus was crucified, they used real spikes and a real spear on his body. He bled real blood and cried real tears. He gasped for each breath of real air until, finally, his lungs pressed out his final breath. He left loose ends in his relationships: a mother who stood there watching him die, disciples who wondered what to do next, and siblings who still wondered about his claims of being the Messiah. In addition, Jesus experienced complete separation from God. On the cross he cried out, "My God, why have you forsaken me?" Jesus descended to the lowest parts of death and stood in consummate separation from God. And in that position he claimed death and hell as his own.

> **Death will still be an annoyance to us, but it can no longer make good on its most sinister threats.**

Because Jesus has done this, we believers can't remain content to tell spooky stories about the power of death and hell. Jesus has deposed death and hell and has exposed them as they are: powerless, weak, and under his control. Death is impotent and has no final power in itself. In this way, Jesus exposes the powerfulness of God and his love. Death will still be an annoyance to us, but it can no longer make good on its most sinister threats.

In Jesus' death and resurrection, his body was reconstructed into an eternal glorified body. His friends were reunited with him in heaven, and the separation he experienced from the Father was completely overcome when he took his place on the throne at God's right hand.

For us believers, our life is in Christ. Our death has already unfolded in him. In him, we have been separated from God, and in Christ, we have been re-united, with our position in eternity already sealed. We will not taste the second death. At the time of our physical death we'll immediately move from this body into our spiritual body. We will move from knowing *about* God to *seeing him,* face to face. We will move from physical life, through physical death, into eternal life.

Because of Christ, we already have these things as unrealized possessions. Through understanding death, we can better live our lives as we keep growing in Christ. Finally, within ourselves—and with all persons we meet in our daily lives—we can keep raising the most important question about death: *Are you ready to live?*

READERS' GUIDE

For Personal Reflection
or Group Discussion

INTRODUCTION TO
THE READERS' GUIDE

The Questions for Life series gets to the heart of what we believe. Sometimes our own mortality sort of smacks us in the face and we find we are afraid to die. *What Happens When I Die?* is a question that haunts everyone at some point in life. As you read through this book, use the discussion points in the following pages to take you to another level. You can study these points on your own or invite a friend or a group of friends to work through the book with you.

Whether you are just checking God out or desiring to go deeper in your relationship with him, let yourself be challenged to change the way you live based on the answers you discover to life's most pressing questions.

Chapter 1: Can death die?

1. To what extent do you fear death? When has that fear been most powerful in your life?

2. How different will "meeting Christ" be for the believer and the nonbeliever?

3. Can you identify with any of the false assumptions people believe about the afterlife? What new insight has changed some of your own assumptions?

4. What is the paradox about where sinners spend eternity and where "good" people spend eternity?

5. What causes the ultimate disconnect of our lives? How have you experienced this?

Chapter 2: What's on the bottom of Jesus' feet?

1. According to Psalm 110:1, what is Jesus putting his feet upon (in answer to this chapter's question)?

2. What confidence do you gain, knowing Christ is seated in ultimate authority?

3. Why do you think we are always so quick to blame others for our own mistakes? When have you seen this in action? What can we do about it?

4. What makes the act of baptism so powerful? If you've been baptized, talk about how it affected you. What is its impact today?

5. How far-reaching is the impact of your life? Is it temporary or eternal? Explain.

6. What do we carry that allows us to face life's challenges? How could you apply this to your own tough times these days?

Chapter 3: What happens sixty seconds after I die?

1. What did Thomas learn about our new bodies when he saw Jesus after the resurrection?

2. How does it make you feel, knowing that we will give an account to Christ of our motives, thoughts, and decisions?

3. Talk about some of the ways you are developing your talents and abilities to impact the lives of others. In what ways are you doing this?

4. What will be the determining fact of our lives for "passing the test"? What are your reasons for thinking you'll pass? Can you back them up with biblical truths?

5. How dependable have you been with what Christ has given you? Share some examples before considering: What are some ways you could *increase* your faithfulness?

Chapter 4: How will I know if I'm dead?

1. What do you most look forward to about your new body?

2. What parts of God's character do you wish people would exhibit now?

3. What makes our new bodies grieve?

4. Do you think we will be idle in heaven? What work will we have to do?

5. What purpose is left to be fulfilled in heaven?

Chapter 5: Can we talk to the dead?

1. Why are people so interested in talking to the dead? Have you ever been tempted to do so?

2. What is your impression of people on television who claim to talk to the dead?

3. In what ways have you seen people deceived by their false beliefs about this?

4. What are some of the deceptions our generation believes about the afterlife? How would you speak to them about it?

5. What are some of the dangers of trying to talk to the dead?

6. What happened when Saul ignored the prohibitions about consulting mediums and psychics? How does this event apply to our lives today?

Chapter 6: Why die twice?

1. What will happen when God has his way in the three places discussed in this chapter?

2. Describe some of the things that will be missing in heaven.

3. Do you think some people actually *choose* hell over heaven? Why would they do this?

4. How was Jesus' philosophy of death different than ours today?

5. Have you received the life of Christ so that you won't have to die twice? Describe that moment.

NOTES

1. A. F. Kirkpatrick, ed., *The First Book of Samuel* in The Cambridge Bible for Schools and Colleges (Cambridge: University Press, 1911), 245.

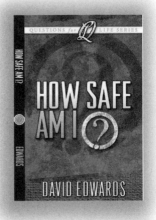
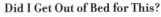

Answers to Life's Tough Issues from the Questions for Life Series

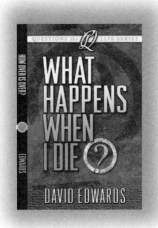

What Happens When I Die?
Killing Your Fear of Death

ISBN: 0-78144-141-2

Why Is It Taking Me So Long to Be Better?
Renovating a Life Like Yours

ISBN: 0-78144-140-4

Why Is This Happening to Me?
Understanding Why You Suffer

ISBN: 0-78144-138-2

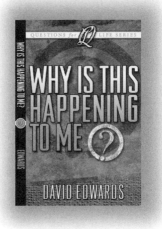

About the Author

David Edwards travels the country full time, speaking to over 200,000 young adults each year in churches and a variety of other settings. As a member of Generation X, he knows firsthand the conflicts, passions, and dreams of this generation.

He has been a featured speaker for citywide weekly Bible study groups in eight states and has authored the Destinations video series as well as his books *One Step Closer* and *Lit*. By addressing the real issues and struggles of today's young adults, Edwards offers direction to generation searching for answers.

The Word at Work Around the World

A vital part of Cook Communications Ministries is our international outreach, Cook Communications Ministries International (CCMI). Your purchase of this book, and of other books and Christian-growth products from Cook, enables CCMI to provide Bibles and Christian literature to people in more than 150 languages in 65 countries.

Cook Communications Ministries is a not-for-profit, self-supporting organization. Revenues from sales of our books, Bible curricula, and other church and home products not only fund our U.S. ministry, but also fund our CCMI ministry around the world. One hundred percent of donations to CCMI go to our international literature programs.

CCMI reaches out internationally in three ways:

• Our premier International Christian Publishing Institute (ICPI) trains leaders from nationally led publishing houses around the world.

• We provide literature for pastors, evangelists, and Christian workers in their national language.

• We reach people at risk—refugees, AIDS victims, street children, and famine victims—with God's Word.

Word Power, God's Power

Faith Kidz, RiverOak, Honor, Life Journey, Victor, NexGen — every time you purchase a book produced by Cook Communications Ministries, you not only meet a vital personal need in your life or in the life of someone you love, but you're also a part of ministering to José in Colombia, Humberto in Chile, Gousa in India, or Lidiane in Brazil. You help make it possible for a pastor in China, a child in Peru, or a mother in West Africa to enjoy a life-changing book. And because you helped, children and adults around the world are learning God's Word and walking in his ways.

Thank you for your partnership in helping to disciple the world. May God bless you with the power of his Word in your life.

For more information about our international ministries, visit www.ccmi.org.

Additional copies of *WHAT HAPPENS WHEN I DIE?*
and other NexGen titles are available
from your local bookseller.
Look for the other books in the Questions for Life series:

WHY IS IT TAKING ME SO LONG TO BE BETTER?
DID I GET OUT OF BED FOR THIS?
HOW SAFE AM I?
HAS GOD GIVEN UP ON ME?
WHY IS THIS HAPPENING TO ME?

If you have enjoyed this book,
or if it has had an impact on your life,
we would like to hear from you.

Please contact us at:

NEXGEN BOOKS
Cook Communications Ministries, Dept. 201
4050 Lee Vance View
Colorado Springs, CO 80918
Or visit our Web site: www.cookministries.com

NEXGEN®

Building the New Generation of Believers